I0644698

ROMANTICISM

THE BASICS

Romanticism: The Basics provides a concise overview of the study of Romanticism and its global dimensions, covering the major aspects of romanticism, from the historical period (1780s–1830s), to different national romanticisms.

It examines the main topics of current scholarly debate with accessible surveys, highlighting both important literary works and exciting recent discoveries of works previously forgotten. Chapters cover different Romanticisms, revolution, empire, race, gender identity, the gothic, science and history, and the Regency. Each chapter uses specific writers to illustrate controversies or debates, as well as surveying a spread of writers, intellectuals, political actors, and innovators whose contributions were indispensable to the period. It also features a helpful timeline, end-of-chapter further reading suggestions, and a comprehensive glossary.

This practical guide to Romanticism offers an expert overview and reveals exciting aspects of recent and current research in the field. It is an essential read for students, scholars, and critics of the Romantic era.

Elizabeth A. Fay is Professor of English Emerita at University of Massachusetts Boston, USA. She is the author of seven books on Romanticism: *Becoming Wordsworthian: A Performative Aesthetic* (1995); *A Feminist Introduction to Romanticism* (1998); *Romantic Medievalism: History and the Romantic Literary Ideal* (2002); *Fashioning Faces: The Portraitive Mode in British Romanticism* (2010); *Romantic Egypt: Abyssal Ground of British Romanticism* (2021); and *Afterlives of Frankenstein: Afterlives of Frankenstein* (2024).

The Basics

The Basics is a highly successful series of accessible guidebooks which provide an overview of the fundamental principles of a subject area in a jargon-free and undaunting format.

Intended for students approaching a subject for the first time, the books both introduce the essentials of a subject and provide an ideal springboard for further study. With over 50 titles spanning subjects from Artificial Intelligence to Women's Studies, *The Basics* are an ideal starting point for students seeking to understand a subject area.

Each text comes with recommendations for further study and gradually introduces the complexities and nuances within a subject.

ELT
MICHAEL MCCARTHY AND STEVE WALSH

LITERARY THEORY (FOURTH EDITION)
HANS BERTENS

SHAKESPEARE (FOURTH EDITION)
SEAN MCEVOY

POETRY (FOURTH EDITION)
JEFFREY WAINWRIGHT

SEMIOTICS (FIFTH EDITION)
DANIEL CHANDLER

LANGUAGE (THIRD EDITION)
ANDREEA S. CALUDE

SPEECH AND LANGUAGE THERAPY
SEAN PERT

ROMANTICISM
ELIZABETH A. FAY

For a full list of titles in this series, please visit www.routledge.com/The-Basics/book-series/B

ROMANTICISM
THE BASICS

Elizabeth A. Fay

Routledge
Taylor & Francis Group
LONDON AND NEW YORK

Designed cover image: The Great Red Dragon and the Woman Clothed with the Sun (c. 1805) by William Blake

First published 2027

by Routledge
4 Park Square, Mi ton Park, Abingdon, Oxon OX14 4RN

and by Routledge
605 Third Avenue, New York, NY 10158

Routledge is an imprint of the Taylor & Francis Group, an informa business

British Library Cataloguing-in-Publication Data
A catalogue record for this book is available from the British Library

ISBN: 978-1-032-62568-3 (hbk)
ISBN: 978-1-032-62569-0 (pbk)
ISBN: 978-1-032-62574-4 (ebk)

DOI: 10.4324/9781032625744

Typeset in Bembo
by Deanta Global Publishing Services, Chennai, India

CONTENTS

INTRODUCTION: WHAT IS ROMANTICISM?

INTRODUCTION: ROMANTICISMS

Romanticism is a historical period when referring to a national expression of its spirit: British romanticism, Italian romanticism, German romanticism, etc.. This volume will focus on the British Romantic period, which spans from the 1780s to the 1830s, but it is important to understand the history and culture of the period within the context of romanticisms, particularly romantic movements in Europe, North and South America, the Caribbean, and India. What unites these different romanticisms is a belief in the individual's right to liberty, accompanied by a belief in individual will, genius, and agency, and in the importance of the imagination and intuition rather than empirical knowledge in determining a future. This view of the individual's ability to shape their future encourages experimentation in the arts, the sciences, industry, exploration, and technology. It is also uncomfortably allied with colonialism and the state's capacity to shape *its* future through expansion, trade, and war.

The difference between a monarch's expansion of their kingdom and colonial expansion is the role of **the individual**: in the latter, individuals are pursuing their own goals for their own good. This is Adam Smith's economic theory of how individuals can jointly affect a national good from the bottom up. Therefore, capitalism cannot be separated from political rights when studying the Romantic period. Although economic theory is not one of the topics discussed, its role in imported goods, the increasing

DOI: 10.4324/9781032625744-1

production of commodities, and the rise of consumer culture underlies much of what concerns the chapters that follow. Without that impetus, the Atlantic trade in enslaved persons, the importance of sugar to the British economy, the relative value of cotton fabrics from India (known as Hindustan), tea and porcelain from China, and opium from Turkey and China would not have had the importance they did for how people experienced their lives and interpreted other cultures. These and other aspects of the new consumer society that accompanied the rise of romanticism were related to the increase in leisure pursuits (Campbell 44). Imagining romanticism without capitalism would be like imagining a world today without Disney: finance, global trade, consumerism, and pleasure were laced together with a romantic aesthetic in a similar way. This period's love affair with consumerism was only possible with the capitalism that brought culturally mixes to London, and other port cities like Bristol and Liverpool, and centers of learning in the north like Edinburgh. So, the topics discussed as "romantic" must be understood as supported by capitalism or its direct result, or – as in the case of abolishing the enslavement of peoples – the political will to elevate human rights over individual profits. Like empire and politics, gender expression was, as now, deeply intertwined with the capitalism and liberalism that made "the individual" a hallmark of romantic thought.

Romanticism was also concerned with **aesthetics**, which theorizes how humans subjectively respond to beauty, whether this is in nature, art, or literature (Bowie 16). The beauties of Shakespeare's verse plays, for instance, were considered as essential to an educated person's taste, as was love of nature. And traveling to beautiful or sublime locations in nature expressly to take the view became an important leisure activity. "**Nature poets**" such as William Wordsworth and Samuel Taylor Coleridge concerned themselves with writing about the imaginative interplay of natural beauty and subjective experience (Hartman 34). Their poetry encouraged the educated classes to use love of nature as another indicator of good taste.

Finally, romanticism is most often associated with the imagination. For the romantics of any nation, use of the imagination as a creative act balanced the demands of reason. While **Reason** was the main rallying cry of the 18th-century's tremendous gains in the sciences and other fields of knowledge, romanticism is characterized by the **Imagination**. Perhaps this is why we tend to value romantic works of literature and art over other achievements of the period, regardless of whose romanticism it is.

BRITISH ROMANTICISM VERSUS ROMANTICISMS

The Romantic period in Britain was an age of experimentation in ideas, genres, politics, science, geography, and gender roles. "Romanticism" conveys the relation of British intellectual and cultural life during this period to romantic political and intellectual movements in other nations and cultures, either nearly concurrently (as with German romanticism) or at later time periods (as with 19th-century French and early 20th-century Japanese romanticisms), and through to the early 21st century, with a renewed engagement with William Blake's poetic and visual art.

I will use "romanticism" to refer to the core ideas of individualism, political justice, the importance of the imagination, and the self's relation to nature; the term also refers to national romanticisms such as British romanticism. I will use "**Romantic period**" to refer to the British historical period as opposed to another national romantic period, and "romantics" to refer to anyone engaging a mode of thought we would call romanticist.

German romanticism, with its theorizing of aesthetics, was influential across Europe and Britain with the publication of Goethe's sentimental novels *The Sorrow of Young Werther* (1774) and *Wilhelm Meister's Apprenticeship* (1795–1796), Friedrich Schiller's *On the Aesthetic Education of Man* (1794), and the stimulus of Immanuel Kant's *Critique of Judgment* (1790). British romanticism received an enormous boost from these and other works translated from the German.

American romanticism arrived later in the 1820s–1830s with the **Transcendentalist** School, which shared important concepts with British romanticism like soul sleep and the importance of nature and the imagination, but developed new ideas suited to the American context such as self-reliance and the inherent goodness of individuals.

Transatlantic romanticism refers to the circulation of ideas, texts, and individuals that arose with the increase in shipping possible after the end of the American War for Independence in 1776. For instance, both Thomas Paine and Joseph Priestley fled to the US when their radicalism became too dangerous to stay in London. Many British families had relatives in America from colonial days and later, from business and trading concerns. Ideas and attitudes came with the travelers while books, magazines, and pamphlets came in the packet boats that delivered letters. The spread of ideas took strong enough hold that by the time Ralph Waldo Emerson (perhaps now the most famous of the Transcendentalists) was writing his works, Wordsworth's lyrics were being taught to Boston schoolboys.

Exciting research continues to be done in other romanticisms, several of those due to the enormous influence of Lord Byron's poetry which spread throughout Europe in the 1820s and was influential in British India (Wootton 462, Fhlathúin 573–4). In Italy, the Italian Wars for Independence were spurred by and concurrent with romantic political philosophy, literature (especially poetry), and art. Much of **Italian romanticism** was associated with the poet Giacomo Leopardi, still revered today in Italy, and writers such as Alessandro Manzoni (Luzzi 84). Patriots living in exile, such as the Italian circle centered on Manzoni's activism and the ideas espoused in his poetry and novels. **Romanticism in India** occurred later, mostly as a literary movement: the age of romantic poetry in Hindi is termed the "**Chhayavad**," but there were numerous poets expressing romantic ideas and a mystical engagement with nature in the other languages of India; notably, Mahatma Ghandi's politics of non-violence and truth are a twentieth-century expression of romanticism (Pachori 248). **Polish romanticism** began in the 1820s with the first publication by the galvanizing poet Adam Mickiewicz, and increased with his extraordinary *Forefathers' Eve* (Koropeckyj 171–5). French writers and artists did not break free of the **Classical period**, which extended past Napoleon's reign, until the mid-19th century with the powerful art and literary output of artists like Delacroix, the poet Alphonse de Lamartine, and Victor Hugo. Research is now being done on romanticism in Korea and Japan, both flourishing in the early 20th century. Some evidence indicates that Korean romantic poetry was in reaction to political oppression, whereas Japanese romantic art was in response to Western influences. There have been different efforts to track romanticism as a global phenomenon as ideas of liberalism, individualism, self-expression, and love of nature spread through trade and immigration.

Writers and artists, as well as cultural figures, were highly experimental during this period, willing to take huge risks with their projects, their careers, and even their lives: Mary Wollstonecraft is a good example of this. A woman philosopher, she was born into the lower middling classes and in a time when women were not supposed to participate in the public sphere. Nonetheless, she supported herself through her writing and became renowned as a female political philosopher.

The **public sphere** was defined as belonging to men of the middle and upper classes: it was where political debates, business, and intellectual discussions could take place. The **private sphere** was the proper one for women because it was confined to domestic and interior spaces: the home, shops, and carriages (DiBattista and Nord 5). Women of these classes were expected to confine themselves to conversation, embroidery and sewing, music or drawing, visiting friends, and shopping for cloth, small goods, or books. Certain public spaces were considered appropriate for men and women to spend time together: balls, theaters, parks, and, of course, church.

Wollstonecraft defied these conventions by opening participation in important debates such as those over human rights. Her first important book was the *Vindication of the Rights of Men* (1790), which Thomas Paine followed with his manifesto *Rights of Man* (1791) on the same topic: both joined in the pamphlet war initiated by Richard Price's polemic, *Discourse on the Love of Our Country* (1789). Central to this debate was the radical thinker and scientist Joseph Priestley and the London Corresponding Society, oriented toward a politicized working class (Haywood 7). It was only when she had made her mark this way that Wollstonecraft wrote her most famous work, *Vindication of the Rights of Woman* (1792) (Tomaselli 168–71). But by this time, she had already experienced those aspects of radical culture that she considered crucial to the new individualism. She had traveled to France to witness the French Revolution, had attempted a "**free love**" relationship with the Swiss artist Henri Fuseli and his wife (they refused), had taken a lover – the American businessman Gilbert Imlay – and had a daughter by him. Like most radicals of the day, she believed institutions such as marriage were designed to constrain people's freedom, since they were still a matter of arranged marriages among the aristocracy and upper classes, or a kind of business contract among the merchant classes. Wollstonecraft ended her most radical period after she met William Godwin, the radical philosopher whose work, *An Enquiry Concerning Political Justice* (1793), laid out how democracy and justice for all social ranks could work hand in hand. Eventually they lived together, and after finding herself pregnant again (with the future Mary Godwin Shelley), she and Godwin decided to marry. This late respectability, taken on solely for the sake of her second child so that she did not suffer the same fate as her illegitimate daughter by Imlay, did not erase the radicalism of her previous years (St. Clair 157–78). After her death, it became clear how many risks Wollstonecraft had taken in both her personal and public affairs: despite being recognized as an intellectual of the highest order during her lifetime, the revelations in Godwin's memoirs of her concerning free love, her affair with Imlay, and her suicide attempts turned public opinion against her. From that point on, she was considered the preeminent example of a "**Bluestocking**," a woman who attempted to be educated in the same subjects as men, and who thought too highly of her mind and not enough of the propriety of her body. "Bluestocking" became a label for young women to avoid at all costs; it meant no young man would be interested in them, since men were looking for companions not competitors for wives.

EXPERIMENTATION AND INNOVATION

The 18th century in Britain was an age of great change as increased travel and marine exploration, accompanied by a loosening of **political** strictures on individual liberties after the Glorious Revolution, in which the monarch Charles II had to agree to a more powerful Parliament and Prime Minister and a decrease in monarchical power. This huge step toward a democratic government meant not only greater political freedom for British subjects, but more freedom to entertain innovative ideas, experiments, technological improvements, and exploration. The energy produced by these activities fueled the **Enlightenment**, or Age of Reason. This high point of cultural achievement in Britain, which like romanticism also took place throughout Europe, was highly influenced by French philosophers such as Diderot, Voltaire, and other renowned intellectuals who developed the earlier work of Descartes ("I think therefore I am" is his famous slogan). In Britain the skeptical philosophy of David Hume had a similar impact (Harris 64–5). Hume's work not only challenged and expanded theories of cognition but also caused the German philosopher Kant to extend his theory of the mind's capabilities and limits. And Kant's work was seminal for German Idealism, in which romantic philosophy, literature and art strove to surpass the limitations Kant saw as inherent in the human mind (Beiser 144–5).

In Britain, the scientific experimentation of the Enlightenment was supported by the **Royal Institution**, a society of men trained in the sciences who engaged in lab experimentation. The exciting discoveries made there or by other men, either with university educations or self-trained, continued throughout the Romantic period and included: the chemistry experiments by Sir Humphrey Davy that he popularized through public lectures; the discovery of chemical elements, like the radical thinker Joseph Priestley's discovery of oxygen; the invention of the battery and study of electromagnetism by the self-educated Michael Faraday; the production of the steam engine by the mechanical engineer and chemist James Watt, which was important not just for manufacture but also led to the earliest locomotive and rail services; advances in astronomy with more powerful telescopes, such as William Herschel's; and to the discovery of new astronomical bodies by Herschel and George III, and new comets, such as that identified by Caroline Herschel. This was the period when geology, botany, and other sciences were codified as specific fields, archeology was developing, and exploration by marine travel was on the increase with attempts at reaching the North Pole.

The impact of such work was to stimulate excitement about uncovering the mysteries of nature. Romantics reacted to such clinical analysis that placed reason over imagination by producing works that argued that the imagination had a greater communion with nature, whereas science merely broke nature down into component parts. At the same time, Romantic period culture was enthused by the new ideas and information that experimentation brought. Botany became important to both artists and writers, and Mary Shelley could not have conceived of Victor Frankenstein or his creation without knowing of Luigi Galvani's experiments with electricity on frog legs called the frog galvanoscope. Nor could she have conceived of *Frankenstein*'s frame narrator Captain Walton's project of attempting to reach the North Pole without the real examples of such endeavors.

"TINTERN ABBEY": CASE IN POINT

Tintern Abbey refers to the ruins in Wales that inspired Wordsworth's iconic ode, and which also was the subject of engravings and paintings. Tintern Abbey offers a good example of the romantic mode: Wordsworth's "Lines Written a Few Miles Above Tintern Abbey," which concludes his and Coleridge's revolutionary *Lyrical Ballads* (1798), takes the ruined abbey as a topos of how memory helps shape the poetic personality by reworking both happy and traumatic experiences. Nature is an important mediator in the speaker's reflections, and the poem begins with the sensory impressions of a seemingly timeless place:

> and again I hear
> These waters, rolling from their mountain-springs
> With a soft inland murmur.—Once again
> Do I behold these steep and lofty cliffs,
> That on a wild secluded scene impress
> Thoughts of more deep seclusion; and connect
> The landscape with the quiet of the sky.
>
> *(2–8)*

However, hidden in the ode's subtitle, "On Revisiting the Banks of the Wye during a Tour, July 13, 1798," and hinted at in the poem are specific political references to other kinds of trauma, specifically the French Revolution, but also gesturing to prior political events that likewise upended and ravaged people's lives. The holiday Bastille Day celebrates July 14, 1789, when the feared Parisian prison was torn down by mob anger. Politically informed readings of the poem have noted the muted references in the poem to persons displaced by the French Revolution and Britain's **War with France** that followed. In the natural scene, the speaker finds himself "hearing oftentimes / The still sad music of humanity," but also hints at displacement:

> wreaths of smoke
> Sent up, in silence, from among the trees!
> With some uncertain notice, as might seem
> Of vagrant dwellers in the houseless woods ...
>
> *(17–20)*

Whereas engravings and paintings of the abbey ruins deepened Romantic interest in nature and aesthetics, with connections to landscape architecture in the period, Wordsworth's politicization of the poem links the natural scene to the human tendency to impose suffering on others. Yet this complication of an aesthetic scene allows him to use nature's beauty surrounding a historic building that had been deliberately defiled to gain a larger understanding of the subjective engagement with "Nature," the natural world that is also a divine expression. Partway through the poem the speaker has a transcendent experience of "another gift."

> Of aspect more sublime; that blessed mood,
> In which the burthen of the mystery,
> In which the heavy and the weary weight
> Of all this unintelligible world,
> Is lightened ...
>
> *(38–42)*

Wordsworth's interweaving of a Gothic ruin and others' displacement evokes memories of his own existential crisis in prior years, Nature's beauty, and sublime transcendence, and his concern for the future produces an exemplary romantic text. His more distanced treatment of the abbey ruins, using them as part of nature rather than separate from it, is also romantic, but connects with the fascination with medieval buildings, especially those with violent pasts and superstitious beliefs, that Gothic fiction and engravings of medieval structures such as the abbey exploited. Wordsworth hints at the Gothic with his rumination on the world's heavy and weary weight which is so incomprehensibly ruinous. The Gothic, discussed in Chapter 4, can be considered the underside of the **sublime**. In that sense, with both sublime and Gothic associations working in tandem, both transcendent joy and unbearable darkness, "Tintern Abbey" reflects romanticism as a mode such that it has ready analogues in German, Italian, American, and other romanticisms.

In the chapters that follow, the topics sketched above will be examined more closely: revolution and its association with romanticism; empire and the cultural otherness it creates; gender expression and constraints; the Gothic; the connections between historicity, science, and futurity; and finally, a topic not mentioned above but which pulls together the many contradictions of the period, the **Regency** with its cultural and consumerist extravagances.

SUMMARY

We see that "romanticism" refers to an intellectual and artistic movement, and that romanticism was a dominant cultural expression at different historical periods in different national milieus. We also see that romanticism cannot be understood without certain attendant cultural phenomena such as:

- The elevation of the imagination as coequal or more important than reason.
- The importance of the Enlightenment to romantic thought.
- The elevation of the individual as a subjectivity with agency over the collective.
- A strong consumerist and global capitalist economy.
- A dependency on empire and its colonial effects.

- The importance of the French Revolution to romantic thought generally.
- An atmosphere that fostered scientific innovation and philosophical speculation.
- Feminism.
- An interest in a dark imagination as expressed in the Gothic.
- The rise of aesthetic theory with an interest in discerning the beautiful and the sublime.
- Learning to view and experience nature through nature poetry and the picturesque.

OVERVIEW OF THE BOOK

This book is organized according to the main themes of romanticism as well as topics that highlight the most recent research being done by scholars in the field. Chapter 1, "Revolution and Revolutionary Writers," surveys the importance of revolution as a concept in romantic thought: the individual's importance is itself a revolutionary concept, distinct from a person's status as a subject of the king. This chapter provides a historical overview of the revolutions in the period or significantly impacting it, such as that of the American colonists. Chapter 2, "Empire and Its Others," discusses the significance of empire for romantic thought, which requires cultural others to expand imaginatively. Chapter 3, "Gender Complexities, Gender Expression," explores how gender was expressed more fluidly than we might think in the period, and how this is articulated by writers as well as its impact on romantic thought. Chapter 4, "The Gothic Mode," examines the importance of the gothic to the romantic imagination. Chapter 5 reveals the interconnectedness of scientific innovation and historical thought in "History, Science, and the Future." And Chapter 6 focuses on the final part of the British Romantic period, "The Regency: Social Life, Celebrity, and Literature," an effervescence of the major themes of romanticism in a short span before the shift to a more conservative cultural temper in the following Victorian period.

FURTHER READING

For an overview of the relation between German philosophical thought and British romantic literature, especially poetry, see Mark Kipperman's *Beyond Enchantment*. For a feminist and materialist treatment of romantic treatments of nature, see *Material Transgressions*, ed. by Singer, Cross, and Barnett. For more on Byron's influence on other European romanticisms, see *Byron and Italy*, ed. by Rawes and Saglia. For the importance of new reading audiences to the public sphere, see Klancher's *The Making of English Reading Audiences, 1790–1832*.

WEBSITES

The Royal Institution. https://en.wikipedia.org/wiki/Royal_Institution.

Metropolitan Museum, Art Timeline: "Romanticism." https://www.metmuseum.org/essays/romanticism.

V&A: "The Gothic Style—An Introduction." https://www.vam.ac.uk/articles/the-gothic-style-an-introduction?srsltid=AfmBOoofV6H9XVINd3nKjaAi2BZcFHIjLl8BXOTwI_lziyDGYUmqxdsP.

WORKS CITED

Beiser, Frederick. *German Idealism: The Struggle Against Subjectivism 1781–1801*. Cambridge: Harvard University Press, 2001.

Bowie, Andrew. *Aesthetics and Subjectivity from Kant to Nietzsche*. 2nd ed. Manchester: Manchester University Press, 2003.

Campbell, Timothy. *Historical Style: Fashion and the New Mode of History, 1740–1830*. Philadelphia: University of Pennsylvania Press, 2016.

DiBattista, Maria, and Deborah Epstein Nord. *At Home in the World: Women Writers and Public Life, from Austen to the Present*. Princeton: Princeton University Press, 2017.

Fhlathúin, Máirení. "Transformations of Byron in the Literature of British India." *Victorian Literature and Culture* 42 (2014): 573–93.

Harris, James A. *Of Liberty* and *Necessity: The Free Will Debate in Eighteenth-Century British Philosophy*. Oxford: Clarendon Press, 2005.

Hartman, Geoffrey H. "Inscriptions and Romantic Nature Poetry." In *The Unremarkable Wordsworth*, edited by Alan Liu, 31–46. Minneapolis: University of Minnesota Press, 1987.

Haywood, Ian. "Radical Journalism." In *Romantic Period Writings 1798–1832*, edited by Zachery Leader and Ian Haywood, 6–36. London: Routledge, 1998.

Kipperman, Mark. *Beyond Enchantment: German Idealism and English Romantic Poetry*. Philadelphia: University of Pennsylvania Press, 2016.

Klancher, Jon P. *The Making of English Reading Audiences, 1790–1832*. Madison: University of Wisconsin Press, 1987.

Koropeckyj, Roman. *Adam Mickiewicz: The Life of a Romantic*. Ithaca: Cornell University Press, 2008.

Luzzi, Joseph. *Romantic Europe and the Ghost of Italy*. New Haven: Yale University Press, 2008.

Pachori, Satya S. "The Chāyavād of Jaya Śankar Prasad: An Overview and Evaluation." *Journal of South Asian Literature* 14 (1978–1979): 247–62.

Rawes, Alan, and Diego Saglia, eds. *Byron and Italy*. Manchester: Manchester University Press, 2018.

St. Clair, William. *The Godwins and the Shelleys: A Biography of a Family*. Baltimore: Johns Hopkins University Press, 1989.

Singer, Kate, Ashley Cross, and Suzanne L. Barnett, eds. *Material Transgressions: Beyond Romantic Bodies, Genders, Things*. Liverpool: Liverpool University Press, 2020.

Tomaselli, Sylvana. *Wollstonecraft: Philosophy, Passion, and Politics*. Princeton: Princeton University Press, 2021.

Wootton, Sarah. "Byron and the Victorians." In *The Oxford Handbook of Lord Byron*, edited by Alan Rawes and Jonathon Shears, 462–76. Oxford: Oxford University Press, 2024.

Wordsworth, William. "Tintern Abbey." In *Lyrical Ballads*, edited by William Wordsworth and Samuel Taylor Coleridge, 201–10. London: Henry Frowde, 1911.

1

REVOLUTION AND REVOLUTIONARY WRITERS

INTRODUCTION

"Revolution" and "romanticism" have long been understood as nearly synonymous. "Revolution" signifies a complex of discontinuities from, and transformations of, customary ways of being, thinking, and belonging. In terms of British romanticism, "revolution" refers to political, scientific, ideological, and social shifts in how the present could be construed, and how the past and future should be thought. That is, the individual might now be conceived as more than the sum of their social rank and status, their family and circumstances, and their allegiance to traditional or progressive values. As a result of all these irritations in the social and political fabric of the period, **the individual** came into being as a social entity separable from its contexts and with a future it could determine for itself. The individual, however, could not be thought without a thorough upheaval in the political order, an event brought on in Britain and Europe not by the American War for Independence but by the French Revolution.

"Revolutionary romanticism" and similar terms have therefore long been specifically understood as the cultural response to the historical events of the French Revolution and the horrific Reign of Terror through to the end of the Napoleonic Wars. The American War for Independence, however, is the economic and political background for these transformations in governmental structures and power because the colonists fought for the right to be represented in the British Parliament. Politically, this

DOI: 10.4324/9781032625744-2

meant representation as subjects to the crown, but when extended through new political views such as those propounded by Thomas Paine and others as "**the rights of man**," these transformations would be what allowed the individual to be conceived philosophically, socially, psychologically, and politically. Still, it is a concept bound in gender and class constraints that were loosened but not lost: the individual as such was male, of the middling or upper ranks, educated, and with economic means. At the same time, revolutionary ideas extended to British, American, and European cultures more largely. Therefore "revolution" must also be understood in a much broader context so that it explains experiments in lifestyle, art, literature, and philosophy as well as politics and social justice.

When examined comparatively, the various threads of what in hindsight we can call "romantic revolution," beginning with the French Revolution, can reveal why it was so enormously compelling in promising a new order that would do away with the socio-political and economic structures that kept people despite their talents in the place, trade or occupation, and social status to which they were born. What turned into the devolution of France's great experiment into the **Reign of Terror**, in which ideological clashes between revolutionary parties, the execution of Louis XVI and Marie-Antoinette as well as much of the aristocracy, and anyone suspected of treason against the ruling faction, provided the dystopian counter to the earlier hopes of a revolutionized society.

"Revolution," in other words, connotes both the utopian and dystopian during the period, with intellectuals and artists such as William Blake (1757–1827) and Percy Bysshe Shelley (1792–1822) retaining their fervent belief in revolution's potential even during the Napoleonic Wars and their aftermath. Many conservative politicians and intellectuals were staunchly against the French Revolution throughout, writing tracts, pamphlets, novels, and poetry to reveal any change to traditional structures and institutions as dangerous, self-serving, and hypocritical on the part of the revolutionaries, and deeply amoral. Even the conservative Whig politician Edmund Burke, who supported the American colonists' revolution against oppressive treatment by the British government, came out against the French Revolution. His commentary, *Reflections on the Revolution in France* (1790), was highly influential in painting the French royal family as victims and the Parisian people not as impoverished and hungry due to bad fiscal policy and a bad harvest, but as an aroused rabble behaving with mob fury. Burke was a complex thinker with many liberal views on other subjects, but he derided the French attempt to destroy the social fabric to create a new one. Others were harsher, and the attacks were often focused on those British intellectuals who expressed pro-revolutionary (Jacobin) sentiments such as William Godwin, Mary Wollstonecraft, and others in their circle including the feminist Mary Hays, Thomas Holcroft, and Thomas Paine.

The pamphlet war between **Jacobins** and **anti-Jacobins** was promulgated alongside a visual strain of public commentary and caricatures, and put printshops at the forefront of political debate in the circulation of news, ideas, and ridicule. Caricatures had developed from an earlier print tradition, in which often crude prints were created to illustrate books, broadsheets, and advertisements. Innovations in print technologies meant that by the Romantic period, satiric artists could take advantage of sophisticated techniques to sway public opinion by ridiculing royalty, elites, politicians, foreign events, and particularly the events and aftermath of the French revolutionary period. The visual nature of the often-savage political critique in the caricatures complemented both liberal and conservative verbal discussions of how to understand what was happening in France, and how to reconcile political violence with either traditional or progressive ideas of history and the future. In other words, the French Revolution and its aftermath were a contentious aspect of public life in Britain. The revolution itself acted as a spur to innovations in fields other than the political because of its liberatory promise. Likewise, the following Napoleonic Wars, because they restricted commerce with the continent in both ideas and goods, spurred an already increasing global push for new exploration, commodities, and cultural ideas.

THE BASICS

A brief overview of the American War for Independence and the French Revolution – and the Napoleonic aftermath – will provide context for how those living in the Romantic era experienced life as entangled with, and responsive to, revolution.

Revolutionary events were understood at the time to be associated with influential publications: for American colonists, it was the Enlightenment empiricist John Locke's *An Essay Concerning Human Understanding* (1700) and political philosopher Thomas Paine's *Common Sense* (1776); for the French revolutionaries, it was Genevan philosopher Jean-Jacques Rousseau's *Discourse on Inequality* and *The Social Contract*. Progressive French revolutionaries were inspired by Rousseau's arguments for the individual's right to property and to political representation, but extreme radicals such as Maximilien Robespierre and Louis Saint-Just (the "Archangel of Terror") were equally inspired by Rousseau's appeal to the common good to cleanse the political body of the legacy of monarchical and aristocratic corruption and excess. The American revolutionaries also adhered to the ideas in Rousseau's *Social Contract*, his strongest promoter being Noah Webster, who relied on that work to write his 1785 tract *Sketches of American Policy*, which in turn influenced the outcome of the American Constitutional Convention.

Politically, Britain had fought France on several fronts in the 18th century, from the Seven Years War to hostilities over colonial territory in Southeast Asia, particularly Madras. The **Mansfield Decision** in 1772, in which Lord Mansfield ruled that there was no legal basis for enslavement in England, set the stage to affect the national income from the sugar trade. In short, the British king needed funds, and the American colonists were a ready source, with taxes increasingly applied to raise those funds. What the colonists objected to was being taxed without any way to appeal such bills, or to have a voice in political decisions regarding them. In 1773, the Boston Tea Party was staged to publicly protest the tax on tea and taxation without representation more generally. Two years later the war between the colonies and Britain began in earnest, with France weighing in. General Lafayette famously fought for the colonists, but reciprocally, the British Thomas Paine became both an American revolutionist and a French revolutionist. Although the Declaration of Independence took place in 1776, the war between America and Britain did not officially end until 1783 with the Treaty of Versailles.

The French Revolution did not unfold so neatly, however. It began in May 1789 with a meeting between the king and the

Estates General to consider economic reforms that would address France's financial crisis. The Estates General were comprised of the "First Estate" or aristocracy; the "Second Estate" or clergy; and the "Third Estate" or representatives of the people (which included the increasingly wealthy mercantile classes). It was this last group that felt underrepresented in the meeting, and one month later broke away from the medieval structure of the three estates to form a new National Assembly. Events followed rapidly, with the Storming of the Bastille taking place in July of the same year, the Declaration of the Rights of Man and the Citizen issued, abolition of feudalism, and state control of the Catholic Church all occurring almost immediately. These were the glory days of the revolution, when Enlightenment reason and philosophical visions of self-governance seemed to guide the body politic, and public ceremonies intended to consecrate the new polity, such as the Fête de la Fédération in July 1790, were attended by tens of thousands.

The combustibles that fueled the French Revolution were more incendiary and far more potent than those inspiring the American War for Independence, as subsequent events proved. The French Revolutionary Wars broke out in 1792 after the monarchy lost all ability to contain radical agitation. In 1792, the monarchy was abolished and the French First Republic created, with the execution of Louis XVI in January 1793, and Marie-Antoinette soon after. In June of 1793, another crisis erupted, and the National Assembly was superseded by the Committee of Public Safety led by radical Jacobins and presided over by Maximilien **Robespierre**. This began the Reign of Terror. It is estimated that 16,000 people were sentenced to death by the Revolutionary Tribunal. The Committee was eventually replaced by the Directory, which enabled the rise of Napoleon Bonaparte, an immensely successful military general who became the first Consul of the body that replaced the Directory, the Consulate.

It was a natural step for Napoleon to transform France into an empire, with himself crowned as emperor. From the tremendous turmoil of France's transformations and Napoleon's endeavors as the leading military campaigner to increase its reach through acquisitory wars, Europe experienced a devastation of land, economies, and various struggles for independence from Italy to Spain. The aftermath of the Napoleonic wars – from the Italian

Campaign to the Egyptian Campaign (intended to gain control of trade to the east, especially India), and from the Iberian Peninsula to the March on Moscow – was felt throughout the west as a spiritual and political fall from grace. The utopian forecasts for the French Revolution had resulted in a dystopia of war-torn lands and a broken sense of futurity.

HOPE

Before the dystopia of the Napoleonic aftermath, there was enormous optimism and enthusiasm. Two texts will illustrate the utopian hopes for revolutionary France and the reasons why the American War for Independence was, in the eyes of British radicals, fought on the wrong terms: Helen Maria Williams's *Letters Written in France, in the Summer 1790* for the first, and William Blake's *America, A Prophecy* (1793) for the second.

Williams is an interesting figure because she is essentially the first war correspondent, traveling to Paris with her mother and sister to witness the public celebrations of the French Revolution. Her *Letters* served as eyewitness accounts for events that were understood to be historically significant even as they unfolded. Eventually, she wrote eight volumes of her *Letters*, and her experiences spanned the ecstatic witnessing of the Festival of Federation, the celebration of the unity and harmony of the new political order in France, the nadir of a brief incarceration ordered by Napoleon. At twenty-nine, Williams was an accomplished poet (admired by William Wordsworth at the start of his poetic career), modeling how a talented woman could produce influential work without the aid of a husband and without apology for her gender. What she witnessed in Paris was not just a people celebrating themselves, but also social elites embracing the new order and giving jewels and wealth to the new endeavor.

What she did not notice, however, was that the festivals she attended on this initial trip to France were an event by and for the middling classes, not the street vendors and tradespeople who would participate in the march on Versailles that ended with the capture of the king and queen. And what she makes us notice is that the social elites she so applauds for giving their wealth to the cause had such a disproportionate abundance compared to the many impoverished denizens of Paris. Nevertheless, her enthusiasm is infectious, and it is worth tasting since Blake's poem will offer as strong a taste of the disappointments of a revolution fought on the wrong ground. The *Letters* are also an important counter to Burke's *Reflections*, which tell such an opposite story of monarchical rights and political injustice at the hands of the mob.

"And this repeated I with exultation to myself, this is the National Assembly of France!" she writes at one point. "Those men now before my eyes are the men who engross the attention, the astonishment of Europe, for the issue of whose decrees surrounding nations wait in suspence [sic], and whose fame has already extended through every civilized region of the globe" (Letter VI, 82). Her enthusiasm for this new representational form of self-governing, without a monarch or prime minister, shows that the National Assembly was as enthralling to her as the public spectacles that were intended to create through their very enactment the new regime that was to replace the ***ancien régime*** or old order. "How am I to paint the impetuous feelings of that immense, that exulting multitude?" she asks the "friend" who is the recipient of the letters when attempting to describe the Fête de la Fédération. "Half a million of people assembled at a spectacle, which furnished every image that can elevate the mind of man, which connected the enthusiasm of moral sentiment with the solemn pomp of religious ceremonies; which addressed itself at once to the imagination, the understanding, and the heart!"

But her excesses were not confined to the public sphere. Williams is just as ardent when describing the participation of liberal elites and becomes melodramatically sentimental when relating a domestic tale of *ancien régime* injustices. The first can best be illustrated by the following anecdote:

> Madame Brulart ... , wears at her breast a medallion made of a stone of the Bastille polished. In the middle of the medallion, *Liberté* was written in diamonds; above was marked, in diamonds, the planet that shone on the 14th of July; and below was seen the moon, of the size she appeared that memorable night. The medallion was set in a branch of laurel, composed of emeralds, and tied at the top with the national cockade, formed of brilliant stone of the three national colours.
>
> (Letter V, 79)

The irony of this effusion escapes Williams, who sees the new piece of jewelry as a testament to the lady's patriotism. She says nothing of the wealth of gemstones used to turn a prison wall stone into a glittering symbol encrusted with diamonds, emeralds, and presumably rubies and sapphires. The cockade, the Bastille stone, and the laurel were variously symbolic of the lowest stations of society; to proudly display them dripping in gemstones as aristocratic patriotism is to signal that the new order was expected by the elites to hold a special place for them just as the old order had done. But Williams sees nothing but that such gestures indicate "the highest honour on [one's] humanity," a phrase she uses in the next sentence regarding another aristocrat whose story she then relates (Letter V, 79). A key sentimental tale she narrates later in the volume is one of domestic abuses, the lengthy incarceration of a young man for refusing to marry according to his father's wishes. It is a story that takes up more space in her volume than any spectacle – from Letter XVI through XXV – and of which, she tells the reader, she has special knowledge, concerns an aristocratic family, a baron and his eldest son. This is the emblem for her of *ancien régime* injustice rather than the plight of the peasants and urban poor, or even the situation of the merchant class, with no political representation under the old system.

By contrast, Blake smells hypocrisy and pretension everywhere and finds it especially redolent in the American War for Independence. However, the fault he finds is not with the colonists, whose rage at the British crown he thinks is entirely justified, but with the British forces – king, politicians, and military leaders – who pervert the conflict and ultimately hogtie the new republic's ability to truly produce a free nation. This is the other side of revolution: that the enthusiasm Williams witnesses in Paris with the public celebrations of a new order and the aristocratic embrace of this new regime can be so easily turned against the very people who espouse it. Although Blake does not consider the Reign of Terror's bloodbath and Napoleon's rise and transformation of a republic into an empire to spell the universal failure of revolution, he does clearly see that any revolutionary event can be corrupted from its original intentions through bad actors. The worst actors, however, are not figures like Robespierre but those in whom power is concentrated: his venom targets such as George III, who strove to maintain his grip on the colonies and for whom their loss was considered by some to have caused his developing madness. Blake makes his negative analysis of American independence in an early masterpiece, *America, A Prophecy* (1793). As a work of art, it could hardly be more opposite Williams's *Letters*; of course, it was composed three years later, after the early excesses of the French Revolution had transpired, but it concerned a far different event which Blake viewed in a far darker vein.

In that work he inveighs against George III, imagining him as the bringer of apocalyptic times. In this work, "Albion" is Britain, Bristol is a major port for the trade in enslaved peoples:

> On Albions Angels: then the Pestilence began in streaks of red
> Across the limbs of Albions Guardian, the spotted plague smote Bristols
> And the Leprosy Londons Spirit, sickening all their bands:
> The millions sent up a howl of anguish and threw off their hammerd mail,
> And cast their swords & spears to earth, & stood a naked multitude.
> Albions Guardian writhed in torment on the eastern sky
> Pale quivring toward the brain his glimmering eyes, teeth chattering
> Howling & shuddering his legs quivering; convuls'd each muscle & sinew
> Sick'ning lay Londons Guardian. and the ancient miter'd York
> Their heads on snowy hills, their ensigns sick'ning in the sky.
>
> *(Copy O, pl. 17, 2–13)*

This fiery, torment-laden text denies that revolution can be effective if the spirit sickens. It turns out that the colonial leaders cannot lead the people to a successful outcome if they lose their resolve and dampen the revolutionary fervor of those most affected, the people themselves. As Blake's prophet indicates near the beginning of the poem, "Albion is sick. America faints!" (pl. 6, 5), while in the later portion excerpted above, London's own population suffers from a leprous disease of heart and mind. Among other things, the reference to London is to the traumatic aspect of the war with the colonies in which British soldiers were sent to fight colonial brothers, who were sometimes literal brothers or family members. The "howl of anguish" sent up by the "millions" paints a terrible imagining of what revolution is really like, whether it is fought on righteous terms or not.

The **Abolition** movement provides a distillation of how revolution and liberation were concepts with both progressive aspects and decided backlash. The trade in enslaved peoples was enmeshed with the trade in sugar, molasses, and rum. It was in every sense both an economy of bodies (unpaid labor and paying consumers) and part of the networks of colonialism that includes not only the transfer of large numbers of people from northwestern Africa to an increasingly overpopulated West Indies but also the effects of monoculture practices of Caribbean plantations, which changed the natural resource structure of the land. Through increased commerce in peoples, animals, plants, and goods, the slave trade demonstrates the effects of increasing global markets more generally. Profit-driven commerce, including colonial efforts to increase the economic interests of centers of power (which France held on to as much as did Britain and Spain), worked to decrease people's freedom and well-being – the very opposite of revolution, progress, and liberal intentions. And yet, those who boycotted sugar in Britain were far outweighed by those parliamentarians so keenly aware of how necessary the sugar plantations were to the national economy.

Abolition was itself extraordinarily controversial (discussed in relation to empire in Chapter 2). Two of the leaders of abolitionism were William Wilberforce and Thomas Clarkson. The conservative Hannah Moore was among the group that convinced Wilberforce to take on the cause, revealing that human rights are not a straightforward story. Thomas Clarkson was a friend of William and Dorothy Wordsworth, and although William Wordsworth was an early promoter of the French Revolution, he was soon to lose his radicalism once he settled down to poetry, and he did not devote his poetic endeavors to promoting Clarkson's agenda. In 1807, he did write a tribute to the hero of the Haitian Revolution, "To Toussaint L'Overture," as well as to his friend, "To Thomas Clarkson. On the Final Passing of the Bill for the Abolition of the Slave Trade." But Wordsworth's poems have a personal rather than polemical affect, unlike other writers who used literature to sway public opinion, such as Thomas Day and

John Bicknell's hugely influential 1773 "The Dying Negro, A Poem," which told the true story of a Black man who committed suicide in London, and which sold in the thousands, or Robert Burns's ballad "The Slave's Lament—" (1792). Like many others, Wordsworth experienced a weariness with revolutionary promise that is evident in his poems on the slave trade. The tribute poems do not hide the cost of revolution to those heroes and champions of the events, a cost that many were beginning to be all too wary of.

CONSERVATIVE BACKLASH

In his book on Blake, Saree Makdisi concentrates on *America, A Prophecy* for the way it reveals schisms in British radical circles of the late 1780s to early 1790s, the years in which pro-French Revolutionary sentiment was at its height. We tend to think of those aligned with pro-revolutionary sentiments as essentially the circle of the radical publisher Joseph Johnson: William Godwin, Mary Wollstonecraft, Thomas Paine, Joseph Priestley, and Mary Hays. Most of these figures were **Dissenters** (educated to be more free-thinking) as well as political philosophers. As such, they were equipped to think through the possibilities of reform but not of revolution gone wrong. As Makdisi reveals, their collective vision was for a rational society governed by a rational political system, one that sustained its own conservatism. The emotions such as Blake portrays in his rage and despair filled *America* are the antithesis of a state of Reason – a state that can only be the result of negotiated compromise and careful planning. The American colonists pursued such a path, although their political and legal systems still did not achieve the level of justice Godwin argued for in his signal work, *An Enquiry Concerning Political Justice* (1793), or that Mary Wollstonecraft theorized in her plan for equality in land ownership in *Vindication of the Rights of Men* (1790), or the rights of women to education and salaried work in *Vindication of the Rights of Woman* (1792). Blake would have said the American system was lacking because it suppressed the people's voices, with leaders making decisions for those they pretend to represent.

At the radical extremes were those more aligned with Blake's views, such as Thomas Spence, who came under attack not just from Tory conservatives, as Godwin and his peers did, but from the British government. Spence and other radicals belonged to the **London Corresponding Society**, a collection of debate clubs that closely followed the arguments of French revolutionaries and argued for a democratic reform of parliament (Davis et al xvii–xix). He and other members of the Society were charged with high treason in 1794 at the height of government repression of radicalism, spending seven months in Newgate prison; he was arrested again in 1801 and sentenced to a year in prison for seditious libel. Publishing radical ideas was indeed a dangerous occupation. Blake was on safer ground since his most political poems only circulated among a small group of admirers, whereas Spence was determined to sway public opinion towards abolishing aristocratic ownership of land in favor of publicly owned land, which would solve the problem of increasingly impoverished small farmers who were being turned off the land they worked when unable to make the rent.

If the government attacked radicals like Spence, it was conservative writers who attacked moderates like Godwin and his circle. A pamphlet war ensued between liberals and conservatives; more wide-reaching, though, were the literary attempts of both sides. Jacobin, or pro-revolutionary, novels such as Godwin's *Things as They Are; or, The Adventures of Caleb Williams* (1794), written to illustrate his *Political Justice*, were countered by attacks by anti-Jacobin novels. Godwin's novel illustrates how innocence is no protection against the word of a social superior, and how social and legal institutions can affect one's self-worth. Mary Hays wrote a similarly compelling novel with a female protagonist, *The Victim of Prejudice* (1799). Mary Wollstonecraft was a particular target of anti-Jacobin women writers for her feminist ideas but even moderates such as Elizabeth Hamilton in her novel *Memoirs of Modern Philosophers* (1800), which takes up the revolution debates, urged women's place as strictly domestic.

Wollstonecraft was particularly attracted to the revolutionary concept of "free love," which was intended to counter the constraints of marriage on women's agency, with an attendant lack of legal rights or political representation for women. While this made her vulnerable to attack even after her marriage to Godwin, it was a strong attraction for Percy Bysshe Shelley, who was even more strongly influenced by Godwin's *Political Justice*. When Shelley came to the Godwin house, Wollstonecraft was long dead, but her daughter Mary Godwin became another strong attractor. Convinced that free love was a better relational form, Shelley convinced Mary to elope with him, estranging Godwin. Thus, the liberal philosopher Godwin became conservative in relation to his first wife's feminist convictions, and Shelley carried the torch for revolutionary ideals as apocalyptic and utopian as Blake's. His works, particularly *Prometheus Unbound* (1820), continued to uphold the potential for a truly democratic society, while his most trenchant critiques, such as *Triumph of Life* (1822) revealed the inherent corruption in civil society as it has been known through the ages. Mary Godwin Shelley's most famous work, *Frankenstein* (1818), demonstrates that utopianism will always be undercut by the male ego; the innocent will have no recourse against patriarchal privilege or societal prejudice. The novel combines both of her parents' arguments, Wollstonecraft's against patriarchy and Godwin's against social injustice. Unlike her husband, Mary Shelley could not sustain a faith in revolutionary promise. But nor was she conservative, and her novel *Valperga* (1823), set in Renaissance Italy, positions two strong women characters with philosophical and leadership qualities against a despotic historical figure, Castruccio, Prince of Luccal, who, in some ways, prefigures both the French despots, Louis XVI and Napoleon I.

The cost of revolution must also be considered, and in ways that Mary Shelley's novels reflect. Britain's wars with France lasted from 1793, the year Louis XVI was executed, to 1815, with the defeat of Napoleon at the Battle of Waterloo. The wars began when France's military forces reached Belgium, and national anxiety over a possible crossing of the English Channel was roused (something Napoleon would later re-arouse). The wars continued with campaigns against every instance of France to gain control over trade routes, showing that early on the revolution in France had imperial underpinnings. The cost in trade, however, was tangential to the cost in lives lost, with the battles fought on land and at sea that devastated Britain's male population. This was as much a cost to mothers and wives as it was to young women for whom there were a decreasing number of young men to marry. Women's novels such as those by Jane Austen in *Pride and Prejudice* (1813) and *Persuasion* (1818) represent both the public pride in British military and naval officers, and the battle at home over the few available marriageable men. But the plight of the common soldier and sailor is also the subject of literary treatment. In *The Ruined Cottage* (1797), Wordsworth depicts the widow of a poor soldier who never returns from war, and in other poems we get glimpses of veterans who return missing limbs and, unable to work, fall destitute. Antiwar literature tended generally to focus on the ordinary or middling class man's fate in the military or navy because that was the portion of the reading public most interested in this aspect of the extensive, and seemingly unending, wars with France. As with Blake's critique of the American War for Independence, then, the cost at home to families and loved ones was found to be a very high price, perhaps too high, for a revolution that does not live up to its promises.

WHIGS AND TORIES

Between radicals like Spence, political philosophers like Godwin and Wollstonecraft, and the conservatives were the **Whigs**. This group was the liberal branch of party politics while the **Tories** were the largest group of conservatives. Liberals promoted progress and reform; Tories believed in hereditary land ownership and aristocratic stewardship of the people. But **Whiggism** was understood to uphold the rights of the wealthy elites and so was far from allied with radicalism and its espousal of the rights of laboring men. (Women were understood by all groups to not be worthy of political representation or rights, and although feminists argued strongly for women's right to respect, whether this is a respectable livelihood or domestic safety, these ideas were not shared by most. In any case, feminists confined their arguments to the middle ranks of society.) Whigs were liberal insofar as they opposed absolute monarchy, favoring instead constitutional monarchy and a strong Parliament. They opposed **Catholic Emancipation**, seeing the Catholic Church as upholding medieval traditions and a return to the past; and in a similar vein, they supported the American struggle for independence as a progressive cause.

In the Romantic period, however, Whigs began to struggle for supremacy. During George III's reign, Tories gained prominent positions in government against the Whig party, which responded to this threat by reorganizing with Charles James Fox at its head. The Tories were headed by William Pitt the Younger, Prime Minister from 1783 until 1801, and then from 1804 until his death in 1806; he reorganized the Tory party as "the new **Toryism**," which effectively replaced the Whigs as the reigning political party. Pitt was Prime Minister during the most turbulent years of the French Revolution and Napoleonic Wars, and although he was an extremely competent administrator, he is remembered for his harsh suppression of radicalism.

Whigs, then, were allied by their progressive ideas and against Pitt and George III. At the same time, they were principally the party of celebrity, with Richard Sheridan, Georgiana, Duchess of Devonshire, the Prince of Wales himself, and his mistress Mary Robinson among its stars. Robinson was a poet and actress when the prince fell in love with her stage performance as Perdita in *The Winter's Tale*; his patronage of her was short-lived, but her subsequent literary career owed something to the prestige of their very public relationship. Robinson was a strong Whig for most of her life, with a love of monarchical privilege that was only later overturned when she argued for the rights of women. Robinson serves as a good example of a prominent Whig in that her political views were progressive but not radical. Whigs believed in a constitutional monarchy, not no monarchy. When the King and Queen of France were imprisoned awaiting trial, Robinson wrote heavily sentimental odes imagining their melancholic states. Similarly, her lover of fifteen years after the Prince of Wales dropped her was Banastre Tarleton, a military officer who distinguished himself in the American war, becoming known as "Bloody Tarleton" for his heroic exploits for the British side. At the same time, she was a prominent supporter of the French Revolution. These contradictions are part of the liberal dilemma: how to structure a future that does not entirely reject the past, and how to promote the welfare of others without detriment to oneself.

Nevertheless, Whiggism was also the ideology most open to women's rights, or to women of the middle ranks (the laboring classes were beginning to be considered in terms of political representation, but reform was always intended as serving men only). Mary Wollstonecraft's *Vindication of the Rights of Woman* had at first garnered praise and acclaim. But after her death, the reactionary fear of the French Revolution spreading across the English Channel meant that any radicalism, including feminism, must be rejected and reviled. Wollstonecraft became the figurehead of the "**Bluestockings**," a term for intellectual women that was suddenly a pejorative, indicating a woman's lack of femininity and unfitness for male society. Against this, Robinson could not be silent: in 1799 she published a short manifesto, *Letter to the Women of England*, in which she argued for women's genius, the long lineage of brilliant and talented women, and women's right to self-protection under the law. This last concerns the majority of the piece and is her argument against the patriarchal view long held that women's sexuality is their only worth, and that no woman may defend herself against unwanted seduction or rape (that is the prerogative of a male relative). It is a concise argument for the two main points of Wollstonecraft's *Vindication*: women's right to education and to livelihood, both of which would make them less vulnerable to men's predations. It is a less radical statement of what women are due than that of the French feminist radicals, headed by the playwright Olympe de Gouges, who composed the *Declaration of the Rights of Woman and of the Female Citizen* (1791) in response to the 1789 *Declaration of the Rights of Man and of the Citizen* which, like British reform, imagined only men to constitute the citizenry.

The French Revolution is important not just for how it encouraged people to consider throwing off monarchical rule for democratic representation; the struggle for independence spread from France to Italy, Spain and Portugal, Germany, and Haiti. Of these, only Haiti was successful in avoiding a return to some form of monarchy. France saw the rise of Napoleon as Emperor and his successors, and then the return of the monarchy with Louis XVIII in 1815; Italian and German struggles united their countries from principalities into single entities, but Italian unification resulted in a monarchy in 1870, and German unification in 1871 was even more contested. Haiti, or the French colony of Saint-Domingue, offers the swiftest example of liberation, and the most interesting because liberation in this case meant not just from oppressive political rule but from oppression of the enslaved by their enslavers. The **Haitian Revolution** is known as the only successful revolt by enslaved peoples; Toussaint L'Ouverture abolished slavery (although he restored the plantation system with paid labor when Haiti's economy stalled), and he created a governmental structure with himself as governor. While this was not a democratic structure, neither did it descend into dystopia or monarchy as so many of the other struggles for independence did.

Political dissidents of various lands often found themselves in exile; they discovered London to be a congenial congregating place for sharing and disputing political ideas. Many revolutionary leaders, from Italian and South American to Greek, gained support and even a following during time spent in London. British progressives viewed any struggle for independence subsequent to France's as a good, and foreign radicals found support beyond their fellows in exile. In this way, revolution came to Britain, and especially to an increasingly cosmopolitan London. It was not only fleeing French aristocrats who arrived with no more than the disguising clothes they wore; now it was also revolutionaries and intellectuals who added potent new ideas to the mix of positive and negative political sentiments swirling around the general conception of revolution itself.

Literary authors also stirred up popular support for the causes of leaders who had not spent time in exile like Simon Bolivar, the Venezuelan politician and military leader. Bolivar was widely traveled in Europe, educated and married in Spain, and was well connected. He used his talents and leadership abilities to help his own country Venezuela gain independence from the Spanish Crown, as well as Ecuador, Peru, Panama, Colombia, and finally Bolivia, to which he gave his own name. Heroic, larger-than-life men such as Bolivar recalled heroic figures from the past, and there was a consonance in the popular mind between the great liberator El Cid, who defeated the Moors in Spain in the 11th century. El Cid's heroic feats were brought before the public by Robert Southey, whose 1808 epic poem about the medieval knight – as well as his earlier and timely 1796 epic celebration of Joan of Arc, liberator of France – made it clear that the current times had historical precedent, and that great men and heroes were called for now more than ever. This resonated with the reading public, and writers such as Felicia Hemans celebrated similar liberatory feats with an epic poem: *The Siege of Valencia* (1823), which also concerned driving the Moors out of Spain, the allusion being to Napoleon's control of Spain and Portugal, and Britain's Iberian Peninsula Campaign to liberate those territories. Lord Byron echoed the feats of Joan of Arc but in the Iberian context when he included powerful depictions of men and women at the battlefront fighting the invading French troops in his best-selling *Childe Harold*, Canto I (1812). Sir Walter Scott, who turned from poems of an Arthurian bent to historical novels concerning Scottish heroes and culture, such as his *Waverley, or, 'Tis Sixty Years Since* (1814), concerning the Jacobite struggle in Scotland of 1745 for restoration of Charles Edward Stuart to the British throne (essentially a struggle between Tories and Whigs) and *Ivanhoe* (1819), concerning the Anglo-Saxon struggle to maintain power in the face of the Norman dominance. His novels largely increased the public's taste for imagining heroics, notably pitting traditional British values against destructive forces. Byron is himself remembered for helping Greece in its struggle for independence by supplying arms and lending his influence and money for the cause. Writing about liberation from oppression, he embodied his belief in revolution and died participating in one such struggle.

But Byron, and those who shared his continued faith in the importance of liberation such as his friend Percy Bysshe Shelley, were becoming a rare species by the time of Napoleon's death in 1815. While Shelley continued publishing poems about the nature of oppression and the heroism necessary to resist it, such as "The Mask of Anarchy" (1819) – a response to the "Peterloo Massacre" in which peaceful protesters were attacked by cavalry troops on government orders in August 1819 – and *The Revolt of Islam* (1818) on the systemic oppression of the Ottoman Empire. His works were savaged in the reviews; the 1810s saw a rise of conservatism and Tory political dominance, and literary reviewers skewed to the status quo. Even today his poem about domestic abuse, *The Cenci* arouses controversy for the way its heroine suffers a judicial punishment that readers are made to question, revealing how difficult it was at the time even for an idealist like Shelley to retain a utopian faith in the power of liberatory and democratic ideals.

Throughout the Romantic period, literary responses to revolutionary thought appeared in every genre, from the lyric (William Wordsworth's and Samuel Taylor Coleridge's 1798 *Lyrical Ballads*, published after anonymous war poetry by British citizens had earlier appeared) and epic (not just historical epics already mentioned but autobiographical epics such as Wordsworth's *The Prelude*, c. 1805, and Byron's *Don Juan*, 1819–1824); to stage plays concerning colonialism, enslaved peoples, revolutionaries, and other topical issues; to novels on revolution such as *Obi; or, Three-Fingered Jack* by William Earle (1800), which enthusiastically portrays the heroism required for revolt, and at the other extreme, Leonora Sansay's *Secret History; or, the Horrors of St. Domingo* (1808), which gives a terrifying account of American and French responses to the Haitian revolution. The conservative backlash, in other words, was inextricably woven with radical enthusiasm, and yet conservatives – as in the case of Hannah Moore championing abolition – could also promote liberatory projects. In short, the Romantic period was complex, tumultuous, and shot through with both revolutionary and reactionary impulses.

ROMANTICISM AS A REVOLUTION IN THOUGHT

It might be better, then, to think about the romantic revolution less as a social progression and more as a change in how to think about the world. How broad was the concept of revolution to romanticism? The idea of throwing off the past, combined with reclaiming the past through a new lens (the medievalized Gothic craze in novels and plays; epic poems and historical novels about medieval heroes) was as much a revolution in thought, perhaps, as looking to the new possibilities. Political revolution did not last long as a utopian possibility, however: novels such as *Caleb Williams* and *The Victim of Prejudice* did not offer their protagonists freedom from socio-political or economic constraints but rather showed how they were innocents victimized by the institutions in play. Mary Shelley's *Frankenstein* (1818) and *The Last Man* (1826), which both depict futuristic scientific and technological innovations, also both end in large-scale tragedy and death. Yet, this pessimism about the costs of revolutionary thought has not dimmed the liberatory promise that continues to inform the spirit of romanticism since the 1820s.

That is, revolutionary ways of thinking as an imperative of the romantic spirit means questioning traditional customs and structures, so that everything from lifestyle and **free love** to women's intellect and educational rights, environmental concerns, children's education, children's labor laws, and the rights of the laboring classes, came under scrutiny or experimentation. Even how students were taught at Oxford and Cambridge was criticized, based on what British students abroad were experiencing in the German university system – which focused more on practical training, practical reasoning, and logic – and created the way toward a more liberal educational system. The result was the creation of London University in 1826, now University College London, founded on secular principles with students admitted regardless of religion. Students who did not belong to the Anglican Church, including Catholics, Jews, and Dissenters, continued to be barred from Oxford and Cambridge, but increasingly other educational institutions were being created with ramifications for a society that was incrementally moving from aristocratic to meritocratic norms.

Some of the cultural ways in which revolution was encoded in romanticism included new "liberatory" movements such as environmentalism and vegetarianism (the rights of animals; this small-scale movement led to the Royal Society for the Prevention of Cruelty to Animals, founded in 1824 but championed earlier by Wilberforce whose work for abolition is discussed above). The human rights struggle to abolish the slave trade discussed above, abolition, which finally passed Parliament in 1807, led to the passage of the **Emancipation Bill** in 1833, which finally declared enslavement illegal in all British territories. It cannot be separated, however, from other human rights movements such as limiting child labor hours in the 1820s to the **Reform Act** (finally passed in 1832), which pushed for men of the laboring classes to have representation in Parliament. None of these reforms were accomplished swiftly; they were not revolutionary in that sense. But the repeated efforts toward the rights of the individual, and protections of domesticated animals and the lands encroached on by industrialization (as in the attempts to restrict rail extension in the Lake District, where environmentalism first began) all held the promise of liberation in the Romantic sense. Although women's rights were not secured until the next era, beginning with expansion of divorce in the Matrimonial Causes Act of 1857, its seeds were planted in the Romantic turmoil of rights discourse, and Wollstonecraft's *Vindication of the Rights of Woman* remains a touchstone for feminists today.

SUMMARY

The distinction between "revolution," in the sense of innovation at many levels, and the Romantic era as a revolutionary period, in which monarchies were contested by reformers militating for more democratic leadership, helps us understand romanticism as essentially both imaginatively and politically innovative. This essentially innovative spirit, however, was counterbalanced by conservative trends, as in the anti-Jacobin backlash.

- Revolution in all its senses during this period depends on the central notions of: the individual and the "rights of man" (pertaining first to men, with women's and children's rights held as less essential).
- The French Revolution was the defining overthrow of a monarchy for the period and for the romantic imagination.
- Revolution requires a philosophical base; in England, this was composed of political philosophers such as Joseph Priestly, William Godwin, and Mary Wollstonecraft, who all had a Dissenting backgrounds, and of working-class activists, many of whom belonged to the London Corresponding Society, although some were independent thinkers such as William Blake.
- The Whig and Tory parties fought for control of the government; the divide between liberal and conservative values also

played out culturally, illustrated by the divide between progressive women writers and the backlash against "Bluestockings," or intellectual and literary women espousing non-conservative views.

- As revolution spread beyond France, various wars for independence broke out. Among these wars were revolts by enslaved peoples, although the Haitian Revolution was the only one to result in lasting liberation.
- The two great leaders of revolution were Toussaint L'Ouverture, who led Haiti to independence from France, and Simon Bolivar, the Venezuelan military leader who helped dissolve Spain's imperial hold over its colonies.
- Revolutionary thought finally led to the liberation of all enslaved peoples under British jurisdiction with the Emancipation Bill, passed by Parliament in 1833.

FURTHER READING

For an overview of the early days of the French Revolution see Fraistat and Lanser's Introduction to Williams's *Letters Written in France* and Israel's *Revolutionary Ideas*, especially chapters 3–4. For more on the relative radicalism of English Dissenters versus activists like Spence, see Makdisi's *William Blake and the Impossible History of the 1790s*, and for the role of political enthusiasm in radical activities, see Mee's *Dangerous Enthusiasm*. Schama's *Citizens: A Chronicle of the French Revolution* remains one of the best historical accounts. History buffs will appreciate Geggus's *The Haitian Revolution: A Documentary History*. To learn more about resistance to Spanish dominion, see Almeida-Beverage's *Romanticism and the Anglo-Hispanic Imaginary*. Of the novels and poems mentioned above, the most interesting for an account of the terrifying aspects of revolt might be Sansay's *Secret History; or, the Horrors of St. Domingo*.

WORKS CITED

Almeida-Beverage, Joselyn, ed. *Romanticism and the Anglo-Hispanic Imaginary*. Amsterdam: Rodopi, 2010.

Blake, William. *America, A Prophecy*, 1793. https://www.blakearchive.org/work/america.

Davis, Michael, James Epstein, Jack Fruchtman Jr, and Mary Thale. *The London Corresponding Society, 1792–1799*. 6 vols. London: Routledge, 2002.

Fraistat, Neil, and Susan S. Lanser. "Introduction." In *Letters Written in France*, edited by Helen Maria Williams, 9–50. Peterborough: Broadview, 2001.

Geggus, David, ed. *The Haitian Revolution: A Documentary History*. Indianapolis: Hackett, 2014.

Israel, Jonathan. *Revolutionary Ideas: An Intellectual History of the French Revolution from The Rights of Man to Robespierre*. Princeton: Princeton University Press, 2015.

Makdisi, Saree. *William Blake and the Impossible History of the 1790s*. Chicago: University of Chicago Press, 2003.

Mee, Jon. *Dangerous Enthusiasm: William Blake and the Culture of Radicalism in the 1790s*. Oxford. Clarendon Press, 1992.

Sansay, Leonora. *Secret History; or, the Horrors of St. Domingo*. Edited by Michael J. Drexler. Peterborough: Broadview Press, 2007.

Schama, Simon. *Citizens: A Chronicle of the French Revolution*. New York: Vintage, 1990.

Williams, Helen Maria. *Letters Written in France, in the Summer 1790*. Edited by Neil Fraistat and Susan S. Lanser. Peterborough: Broadview, 2001.

2

EMPIRE AND ITS OTHERS

INTRODUCTION

One of the main ways to understand Britain, France, and Spain during this period is through the relation of each of these empires to its colonies, particularly in the Caribbean and South America, including the trade in enslaved peoples. For Britain, the East India Company's colonization of major parts of the Indian subcontinent was an essential part of this colonial spread. These are economic relations, empire as trade routes rather than land acquisition, and colonization as a business venture. In this sense, economic trade is different from the explorations for both scientific knowledge and to claim land for the king, as in the three voyages of Captain Cook. Cook's first two voyages were at the behest of George III in order to observe the transit of Venus from the Pacific Ocean; the king's own scientific achievement was to observe its transit with his telescope in the Kew Observatory. Cook was also ordered to find if there were an uncharted island in the ocean's middle zone. The third voyage was half scientific – George III wanted Cook to seek an Arctic passage between the Pacific and Atlantic – and half colonial; the king sent British plants and animals to be transplanted to Polynesian islands to extend Britain's agrarian reach.

EMPIRE AS TRADE

The difference between the two kinds of missions that Cook was commissioned with exemplifies how global networks were

DOI: 10.4324/9781032625744-3

imagined: exploration was a way to extend knowledge, and thereby to acquire useful materials, better trade routes, usable land, and labor. The two motives of Cook's voyages are revealed in the third voyage to be aspects of each other. There is a good illustration of how empire was economic rather than political: the primary task of British diplomats and ambassadors to other countries was to smooth difficulties experienced by Britons doing business in that location, either by negotiating with the local ruler or by some other measure. For instance, as ambassador to the Kingdom of Naples, Sir William Hamilton's duties included promoting British commercial interests and aiding British merchants, as well as entertaining travelers from Britain. Although Hamilton became renowned for his interest in volcanoes, ancient Roman archaeological remains, and his collection of ancient Greek vases, his service to the empire established his importance to the age. Similarly, the **East India Company** (1600–1874) began as a business venture but was supported by the crown from the beginning, being sanctioned by Elizabeth I, and by the Romantic period, it had a lobby in Parliament. The company's products made up half the global trade by this period, with exports of Asian cotton, silk, indigo dye, sugar, salt, spices, saltpeter, and tea. They also exported more valuable commodities such as gemstones, as well as porcelain and tea from China, and medicinal commodities such as opium. It also traded in enslaved peoples.

The Company had its own military, used to subdue local uprisings from a populace suffering from starvation in bad harvests and political unrest caused by the earlier dissolution of the Mughal Empire, which ruled Bengal where the Company was located. Throughout its history, France was the East India Company's main rival, making the Company a national concern as both countries, as well as the Dutch and Portuguese, fought for western dominion over eastern ports, trade routes, and resources. But the Company was finally able to establish a monopoly over Asia, from the subcontinent to China. The East India Company was also the purveyor of Asian tea to colonial American tea importers, a commodity monopoly that led to the Boston Tea Party in 1773. Company headquarters were in Leadenhall Street in London, and an 1803 act of Parliament established the East India Dock Company, which built the East India Docks specifically for ships trading with India. By 1806, the Company even had its own college to train clerks to do its business. Writers such as the essayist Charles Lamb, friend of Samuel Taylor Coleridge and Leigh Hunt, earned a living as a clerk in the Company's accounting office. His 1823 essay "Old China" provides an ironic reflection on the British habit of drinking Indian tea out of Chinese porcelain, commodities that provided wealth to the Company's stockholders and officers by giving personalities and motivations to the Chinese figures painted on the porcelain.

Another literary connection with the East India Company took place in Bengal rather than London: the philologist Sir William Jones's translations of Sanskrit poetry. His employment there was as a judge; the British controlled the legal administration in Bengal after the fall of the Mughal regime and made up the court system and judiciary. Jones had been a linguistic prodigy as a boy, and during his career learned more languages, eventually being proficient in eight. In Bengal he became fascinated with ancient Indian history, a far cry from the everyday matter of his duties as a puisne, or lower, judge.

Jones's real achievement was to recognize the connection between the languages in the Indo-European family, arguing that Greek, Latin, and Sanskrit all share a common linguistic root, which he extended to Persian and to Germanic and Celtic languages. To learn Sanskrit, which he needed to more thoroughly understand Hindu law for himself, since he found the court interpreters, Brahmin scholars, too often provided different or contradictory answers. To learn the written language, he studied the *Vedas* with a teacher at the Hindu University of Nadiya, Rāmalocana. He then studied Hindu astronomy as well as Hindu and Muslim legal systems, the local botanical specimens, and Hindu music as well as literature (Patterson 109–11). One of his major contributions to science was his role in establishing the **Asiatic Society**. More popularly, his English translations of the literature inspired the Orientalist strain of Romantic period culture and literature, resulting in poems and novels that imagine life beyond the confines of Western culture. Perhaps as influential as his popular translations of Sanskrit poetry was his treatise *Essay on the Arts called Imitative* (1772) in which he argued for expressive poetry rather than descriptive or, as was still popular from the previous period, imitative verse. Poets such as Coleridge and Wordsworth were influenced by Jones, but so were American fiction writers, including Edgar Allan Poe.

EMPIRE AS AESTHETIC: "ORIENTIALISM"

"**Orientalism**" refers to the literary or artistic representation of Eastern cultures in which an expressive, sensuous environment and situation rather than a realistic, accurately described one is at play. Although the term and the concept it represents are those of a white supremacist attitude of a growing empire toward the East in general as its cultural "other," it is important in understanding how the British viewed their relations with Eastern cultures aesthetically as opposed to financially. For the Romantics, this aesthetic provided a dream-like way to imagine life differently; a life in which aspirations could be displaced by sensuous luxury, and sensuousness could be a source of inspiration rather than of historical or factual knowledge.

Orientalism was a highly influential aspect of colonialism rather than its result. From a colonial perspective, the colonized culture typically would be suppressed or forcibly translated into a Western view of cultural heritage and traditions; however, the imperial other, especially the Ottoman Turks, could not be forced into a Western appropriation. The British, for instance, forced colonial change in India, the Portuguese and Spanish in Latin and South America, the French in Haiti (St. Domingue), Algeria, and elsewhere in Africa. But they could not do the same for a rival or superior empire such as the Ottoman. Another way to translate and appropriate a culture was available, however: an aestheticization of that foreignness into something both exotic and yet seductively familiar in terms of the desire it represents. Orientalism was not located in a specific culture, time, or place: the aesthetic it conveys applied to the Ottoman Empire, the Persian Empire, the Indian subcontinent, the Holy Lands, and contemporary Egypt alike, with a similar aesthetic translation of Chinese and Japanese culture and traditions. It was applicable to Eastern cultures rather than all colonized or cultural others; for instance, cultures of Africa (with the exception of Egypt and other Muslim cultures), the Caribbean, and the Americas were not viewed with a similar sense of romance and mystique, ahistoricity, and a sensually inflected cultural languor and embodied desire.

One of the main inspirations for Orientalism was the anonymous translation into English of the *Thousand and One Nights, Arabian Nights' Entertainments* (12 vols., 1706–1721). Wordsworth recounts the impact it had on his imagination as a boy in *The Prelude*, and it seems most schoolboys had access to a copy of it. An important 18th-century influence was the published travel letters of Lady Mary Wortley Montagu, written in Constantinople while her husband served as ambassador to the Ottoman Sublime Porte: her *Turkish Embassy Letters* were published posthumously in 1763 but they circulated widely in manuscript, and the Turkish elements of her dress that she adapted after their return to England were widely imitated well into the Romantic era.

Another, more contemporary but equally important literary influence was William Beckford's imaginative *Vathek* (written first in French; English translation, 1786). Beckford so completely reimagines *Arabian Night*-like episodes and characters that he changed the tone of British Orientalism from a distanced one to one both titillating and with Gothic elements. A novel replete with nightmarish visions, *Vathek* was both otherly and – at least imaginatively and erotically – familiar. Vathek is a ruler with vast powers and vast resources, but he is single-mindedly focused on satisfying his voluptuous appetites and libertine urges. Beckford had held an enormous party for himself that contained elements of the "palace of the senses" he imagined for Vathek to inhabit, such as foggy perfumed smoke in the great hall that obscured vision but heightened the sense. The Prince of Wales recreated certain aspects of the rooms of Vathek's palace in his miniature pleasure palace at Brighton, the Royal Pavilion. But the connection between Beckford's own outsized imagination and appetites and colonialism is revealed by the source of his enormous fortunes: several Jamaican sugar plantations that provided much of his large annual income, which he used to build an enormous art collection that he housed in his own palace, Fonthill Abbey. The sugar that his over 3,000 enslaved workers produced created the wealth that fed his own appetites. This form of colonial wealth, however, was typically displaced onto middling class Britons who worked in India either for the East India Company or in connection with it. Called "**Nabobs**" when they returned with large fortunes, these nouveau riche were considered vulgar because they had wealth without social rank. Thus, those who stayed at home could distance themselves from the ill effects of colonization, refusing to understand the blood costs of the sugar they consumed or looking down on "Nabobs" as somehow no longer quite British.

However, there was real interest in learning more directly about Eastern literatures and cultures, and one of the primary ways to do so was through historical and modern languages. An Orientalist was a philologist, like Jones, specializing in ancient and modern languages of the Mediterranean Near East. Jones founded the "Asiatick Society," later the Royal Asiatic Society of Bengal, to further such scholarship, and the subsequent founding of other Asiatic Societies at home allowed philologists to study documents provided through connections the East India Company facilitated through its trade networks. Many Orientalists folded the Chinese script into their study as they did ancient Hebrew, since part of the philologist's goal was to find a common translative mechanism among language groups. But because Orientalism evoked a generalized sense of the East, particularly the Near East, the evocation was of a timeless culture that was both ancient and contemporary. It took attributes largely from the Ottoman Turkish culture: harems, honor killings, hashish consumption, coffeehouses, arbitrary violence, enormous luxury, and decadence for the ruling classes. Because the last was also an aspect of British culture during the Regency, Orientalism provided a familiarity for readers and theatergoers and a screen for criticism of Britain's ruling classes for perceptive audiences. Lord Byron's Turkish Tales fall into the first category but can be read as critical texts as well.

Byron's first, masterful Turkish Tale was "The Giaour" (1813). The poem replicates the partially heard conversations taking place in a Turkish coffeehouse while narrating the story of a Venetian adventurer whose love for the youngest wife in a nobleman's harem causes her husband to commit an honor killing which the giaour (non-Muslim) heroically avenges. Although the plot is that of a romance, the poem is laden with sensuous detail and language, and the sexuality associated with harems provides the titillation readers associate with Orientalist literature and art. But Byron goes further, creating a realistic portrait of Islamic culture through deep research that he cites in footnotes throughout the text. Although the portrait is that of Near Eastern culture during the height of the Venetian Republic, whose wealth derived from trade with these lands, the culture Byron depicts is the same as that in most Orientalist texts. The historical details get subsumed into the sensuality that readers and audiences wanted from such texts.

Samuel Taylor Coleridge, for instance, deliberately generalizes the Orient in his poem set in Mongol China, "Kubla Khan" (c. 1797; it was Byron who insisted the poem be published in 1816) (for dating, see Holmes, 165). Set in 13th-century China, it includes an important dream vision of an "Abyssinian maid" who could be from anywhere in the contemporary East. Her song inspires both longing and creativity in a way that is highly sensualized. Her song is the poet-speaker's inspiration for composing his own song – but only if he could hear it again. The Orient is addictive, in other words. No one analyzed this addictive quality or the inspirational visions associated with it more than Thomas De Quincey, who wrote *Confessions of an English Opium-Eater* in installments in 1821 purportedly to document how he became addicted to laudanum, the widely available opium liquid that was used for medicinal purposes and was imported from Turkey and China (which led to the Opium Wars in which Britain tried to insist on maintaining a lucrative trade, with the Chinese as both providers and consumers of the drug). De Quincey was convinced that unlike the easterner, addicted to sensuous things, he as a Briton could use willpower to cure his addiction. The *Confessions* attests to the uselessness of willpower in the face of an addictive substance like opium, but it also contains descriptions of the hallucinations that both inspired and terrified De Quincey. In several opium dreams the furniture in his room gains crocodile features while in a horrible nightmare he dreams he is the sacrificial victim for an ancient religious ritual. He recalls that during his darkest period, described in "The Pains of Opium" section, that: "The cursed crocodile became to me the object of more horror than almost all the rest. I was compelled to live with him, and (as was always the case almost in my dreams) for centuries" (May 1818). The monstrous crocodile comes to stand in for the Orient itself in these nightmares. But equally, space and time fall away or merge in the dreams so that: "Space swelled, and was amplified to an extent of unutterable infinity. This, however, did not disturb me so much as the vast expansion of time; I sometimes seemed to have lived for 70 or 100 years in one night; nay, sometimes had feelings representative of a millennium passed in that time, or, however, of a duration far beyond the limits of any human experience" (68).

But writers and artists were also compelled to put themselves into the place of those indigenous to lands being colonized. In these works, the political critique was more obvious and was the main reason for readerly interest. A genre in which Britain is viewed by Oriental others was popular in the 18th century with works like Oliver Goldsmith's *Citizen of the World* (1760), a fictional series of letters by Lien Chi, a Chinese visitor to England who is bemused by British customs and behavior. In contrast, works by actual visitors from the East were sometimes translated into English such as *The Travels of Mirza Abu Taleb Khan*, a three-volume work published in 1814, or were written in English such as *The Travels of Dean Mahomet* (1794). These works offered a more accurate idea of how British culture and manners appeared to non-Westerners.

The *Travels of Mirza Abu Taleb Khan* is a travelogue of the Indian poet-scholar Abu Talib, whose impressions of London at the turn of the century are especially revealing. Having traveled from India to Africa, and then on to Britain and France, his perspective was well-informed but also incisive. He is candid about the imperial nature of British, and especially London, society. And his observations offer a stark contrast to the Orientalist aesthetic by providing a realistic version of Eastern, and specifically Islamic, modernity. The ahistorical, timeless aspect of Orientalist literature and art could not retain its "authenticity," as Byron endeavored to provide in *The Giaour* with all of its footnotes. Instead, Abu Talib provides his learned observations to contrast European modernity with Islamic cultural realities.

Moreover, his informed observations expose the infirmities of British finance – the underpinnings of the empire:

> The public revenue of England is not, as in India, merely raised from the land, or by duties levied on a few kinds of merchandise, but almost every article of consumption pays its portion... Since the commencement of the present war, a new law has been framed, compelling every person to pay, annually, a *tenth* of his whole income. Most of these taxes are permanent ... When the Chancellor of the Exchequer discovers that the revenue is not equal to the estimate of the expenses for the following year, he does not increase the taxes ... [but instead] he borrows the amount, on Government security, and increases the duty upon some particular article of consumption ... which suffices to pay the *interest* of the sum so borrowed.
>
> (205)

As Abu Talib points out, this financing sleight of hand means that in the end the cost of every good goes up, to be paid by the consumer. Abu Talib's clear-sighted analysis of British finance reveals what citizens do not: capital must come from growth in the colonial and trade periphery for the center to hold.

INDIGENEITY

Factual or more empathetic treatments often located their stories in the Americas in this period, since America was viewed as a new country with immense natural resources available to it and also a land where Indigenous peoples pursued a life much closer to nature than in the East. An important poem in this vein is William Wordsworth's lyric, "Complaint of a Forsaken Indian Woman" (1798).

The headnote to this poem, which gives *Hearne's Journey from Hudson's Bay to the Northern Ocean* as the factual basis for the lyric, explains that:

> When a Northern Indian, from sickness, is unable to continue his journey with his companions; he is left behind, covered over with Deerskins, and is supplied with water, food, and fuel if the situation of the place will afford it. He is informed of the track which his companions intend to pursue, and if he is unable to follow, or overtake them, he perishes alone in the Desart; unless he should have the good fortune to fall in with some other Tribes of Indians. It is unnecessary to add that the females are equally, or still more, exposed to the same fate.
>
> (191)

From this cold statement of facts, the reader might not be prepared for the pathos of the first lines: "Before I see another day, / Oh let my body die away!" The lyric is tellingly painful as the poet imagines what it is to be forsaken, ill, and with no hope for rescue. The desolation of the speaker is increased when we learn she is not dying of old age but is instead a young mother: "My child! they gave thee to another, / A woman who was not thy mother" (ll. 31–2). Here the gender complications caused by a female speaker make the Romantic period reader question the trope of the "Noble Savage," a classical ideal of the barbarian warrior that portrays him as the embodiment of Roman virtues, and which was revived in 17th-century British literature. Here the woman faces her death not with heroism but with lament. She complains.

By contrast, Felicia Hemans provides an opposite portrait of a Native American woman heroically going to her death in "Indian Woman's Death Song," complicating Wordsworth's pathetic portrait. In a "light canoe"

> Proudly, and dauntlessly, and all alone,
> Save that a babe lay sleeping at her breast,
> A woman stood. Upon her Indian brow
> Sat a strange gladness, and her dark hair wav'd
> As if triumphantly. She press'd her child,
> In its bright slumber, to her beating heart,
> And lifted her sweet voice that rose awhile
> Above the sound of waters, high and clear,
> Wafting a wild proud strain, her Song of Death.
>
> *(7–15)*

This woman does not complain, she sings proudly her wild "Song of Death." She goes to her death not because of illness, as for Wordsworth's speaker, but because her husband has left her for another woman – a problem more deeply relevant to the British woman reader than to the indigenous woman Hemans imagines. This projection of British values onto a cultural other seems questionable, yet it unquestionably provides stronger empathy for this woman whose bravery makes her indeed noble. Moreover, she takes her infant girl with her into death: "tho' born, like me, for woman's weary lot, / Smile! … I leave thee not" (36–7).

Each of these poems portrays the indigenous woman differently: Wordsworth's speaker is a helpless victim of a terrifyingly patriarchal society, whereas Hemans's speaker is raging against the infidelity of a spouse, unconcerned about how she might have recourse to tribal elders. She does not complain or seek revenge but instead enacts a woman's version of the Noble Savage by acting heroically, a female version of the idealized warrior. These poems then provide the two ways in which cultural others untouched by colonization could be victimized by their own societies, but they also provide the two ways in which cultural others were viewed in general. Abolitionists, attempting to win over supporters to their cause, made plentiful use of both types of appeal: enslaved peoples were either portrayed as helpless victims or as heroically fighting the conditions of their enslavement.

These opposed views can be better understood through the context of how Indigenous peoples were encountered as outliers to empire. England had a long history of encountering North Americans and other Indigenous peoples who traveled or were brought to London. These cultural others were not viewed empathetically but were instead objects of curiosity much like specimens and fossils being brought home by explorers. Most Indigenous peoples brought to Europe and Britain in the preceding decades, even centuries, were treated as a spectacle and put on display. But in 1772 a group of five Inuit people were brought to London from Labrador by the explorer George Cartwright, whose relations with the Inuit peoples were good (he was a seal and fishing trader and depended on them for his business). Instead of being put on display, Cartwright believed a trip to London would modernize these visitors, an educational experience they could use to improve their own culture. This sympathetic endeavor on Cartwright's part, however, was as paternalistic as Wordsworth's female victim; in any case it ended badly when four of the group died of smallpox, and the fifth most likely brought the disease home with her, with disastrous results for her people. In the same period, however, Inuit visitors called "Esquimaux" were being put on display in an exhibition hall, where they could be viewed in their seal skin clothing positioned in front of mockups of their native dwelling. Exhibition posters provide evidence of these and similar spectacles of foreign peoples and animals that were brought to the metropolis in order that Londoners could taste other cultures without the bother of travel. Whereas Cartwright wanted his Inuit tourists to consume British modernity, these displays of other peoples turned them into consumer goods much like Caribbean sugar or Indian cotton. Such attitudes reveal the paradoxes of Romantic era society: a genuine, even scientific curiosity about the non-western world coexisted with an attitude in which the rest of the world was available to consume as a product of global trade and empire. Literature by writers of non-white or mixed race Native Americans is now included in a category that can be termed **Red Romanticism**, after the groundbreaking research by literary historian Tim Fulford.

ABOLITION AND LITERATURE

Unlike the poems by Wordsworth and Hemans, abolitionist works that create Black characters whose woes and pathos are directly attributable to the trade in enslaved peoples – like William Blake's "Little Black Boy" – and the abolitionist movement found greater power in voices of the past expressing suffering, protest, and injustice in texts by those who escaped enslavement. Their narratives have the authority of real lived experience; it was not enough for abolitionists to provide evidence of suffering as a counterclaim to colonial whites' claims to *require* harsh treatment in order to prevent rebellion and ensure profits. The value of *this* singular life made clear in individually voiced accounts was emphatically important to the abolitionist cause; the humanity each such account expresses was necessary for the enslaved and formerly enslaved to be heard as subjects rather than victims. But poems that focus on individual Black figures were important for swaying public opinion in favor of abolition too. And Blake's lyric is exemplary in this regard.

"Little Black Boy," which Blake included in the *Songs of Innocence* (1789) rather than his later *Songs of Experience* (1794), portrays a young Black child whom his mother must help to understand why he will have to experience a life of difference. She explains to her small son that:

> "And we are put on earth a little space,
> That we may learn to bear the beams of love;
> And these black bodies and this sunburnt face
> Are but a cloud, and like a shady grove."
>
> *(Copy L, pl. 8, 15–8)*

Although the child clearly sees that "And I am black, but O my soul is white! / White as angel is the English child, / But I am black, as if bereaved of light" (pl. 8, 2–4), his mother teaches him that this is God's plan and to trust in His providence. Blake's irony in the poem is directed at the hypocritial use of religion – the Black mother is teaching her son what she herself has been taught to believe – to teach enslaved people to tolerate their treatment.
As she explains to her child:

> "For, when our souls have learned the heat to bear,
> The cloud will vanish, we shall hear His voice,
> Saying, 'Come out from the grove, my love and care,
> And round my golden tent like lambs rejoice.'"
>
> *(pl. 9, 17–20)*

Although the mother's teaching is unironic, the pain of a mother who must teach her son such a lesson is palpable.

Other white voices who argued against the trade in African people in more activist ways through lectures, pamphlets, and bills put before Parliament were abolitionists, the most prominent of whom were Granville Sharp, William Wilberforce, and Thomas Clarkson, with the 18th-century philanthropist James Oglethorpe and author Hannah More as strong voices in the movement. Clarkson, a friend of the Wordsworths, helped Granville Sharp found the Society for Effecting the Abolition of the Slave Trade and worked tirelessly to promote the passage of the Slave Trade Act, which was finally passed in 1807, ending all British participation in the trade of captured Africans. (The Slave Trade Act did not end enslavement itself, and the Emancipation Bill, or Slavery Abolition Act of 1833, which ended the practice for British-held lands, was not passed until the end of the Romantic period.) Wilberforce, a Member of Parliament for Yorkshire, together with Granville Sharp and Hannah More, formed the Clapham Sect, an abolition society. Wilberforce was poised to be more effective politically in the arguments put before Parliament, but it required the combined work of both activists and Britons sympathetic to the cause for the Acts to finally be passed.

Joining in these powerful voices of white politicians, abolition societies, and men and women writers were freed Blacks such as Baron de Vastey, Olaudah Equiano, and Ignatius Sancho. Like Equiano and Sancho, Baron de Vastey was influenced by the Enlightenment, with its arguments for the political equality of all men (though not women), and it was an important force in Black humanism. Against Toussaint L'Ouverture's rhetorical promotion of brotherhood across color lines, Vastey, a mixed-race Haitian and Toussaint's contemporary, critiqued colonial dependencies on enslaved workers (Daut 68–9). The slave trade and the high morbidity of the enslaved labor, Vastey unceasingly argued, revealed that a free market economy is merely an ideological justification for the inexcusability of racism (95). Ignatius Sancho, an 18th-century Enlightenment figure like Equiano, was another remarkable contributor to a cultural acceptance of Black liberty. While still enslaved, he was befriended by John Montagu, 2nd Duke of Montagu, who taught him how to read and encouraged his literary interests. He finally escaped the family he was enslaved by in Greenwich and took refuge at Montagu House in Blackheath, London; he served the family as butler for two years before he left to begin his own business as a London shopkeeper. Becoming successful and well-known in Mayfair, Sancho turned his literary interests toward writing essays, plays, and books that furthered his renown. As a property owner, he became the first Black man of African descent to vote.

Olaudah Equiano also became a successful author and abolitionist after escaping enslavement. In his autobiography, he expresses his subjectivity in a manner closer to that of Mirza Abu Talib Khan and Baron de Vastey than to those who wrote escape narratives, although his autobiography covers the years of his capture and enslavement. Like Abu Talib and Vastey, Equiano was of aristocratic class before being captured as a child by African "**slavers**." Equiano was taken from his home in what is now Nigeria, and once in the Caribbean, he was sold to an English Royal Naval officer. This proved fortunate, for as cabin boy, he was treated more favorably than he would have been as a plantation worker. Equiano was both highly intelligent and lucky enough to be taught to read and write; although he was sold three times as a boy and young man, he was so capable that he became a trading partner of his final master and was able to purchase his freedom. His writing is that of an Enlightenment gentleman, eloquent and reasoned, both in his best-selling autobiography, *The Interesting Narrative of the Life of Olaudah Equiano* (1789), and in his political writings published in newspapers. He became a major figure in British abolition, with lectures in the 1780s on abolishing the slave trade, the popularity of his autobiography, and his work to aid poor Black people living in London, most of whom had fought for the British during the American War for Independence, as well as their families.

Another Black writer whose autobiography contributed powerfully to Emancipation, the second stage of the abolition movement, was that of Mary Prince. Her narrative, *The History of Mary Prince* (1831), was the first to be authored by a Black woman, but unlike Equiano, hers was written after a life of painful, torturous treatment and debilitating work. And unlike Equiano's reasoned narrative, Prince's describes the pathos of Black lives in enslavement, with emphasis on how Black women's lives were additionally harrowing because of their sexual vulnerability. But it is her focus on the distress of Black mothers who must see their children sold away from them that powerfully affected British readers. Prince's account of the end of childhood, when her enslaver sends her to work at another house, is charged with the distress of the 12-year-old girl; but the moment when her mother has to take her and her sisters to the slave market to be sold after the death of her enslaver, despite the distance of years at the time of writing, is suffused with emotional pain at confronting this final separation from family and home. Beginning with the day before, she writes:

> Oh dear! I cannot bear to think of that day, – it is too much. – It recalls the great grief that filled my heart, and the woeful thoughts that passed to and fro through my mind, whilst listening to the pitiful words of my poor mother, weeping for the loss of her children.
>
> (3)

In describing the next morning, Prince uses funereal language to depict the emotional death she and her mother feel at this moment: "The black morning at length came … whilst she was putting on us the new osnaburgs in we were to be sold, she said, in a sorrowful voice, (I shall never forget it!) 'See, I am *shrouding* my poor children; what a task for a mother!'" (3). This chilling moment, in which the mother has to sell her own children at the slave market, is heart-rending in itself, while Prince's use of language and word choice feels authentic rather than rhetorically distant ("I shall never forget it!"); the imagery of a funeral rather than a marketplace symbolizes the death of the subject-self that being sold is meant to create. But the exclamations and the never-forgotten emotion reveal, just as surely, that Prince has held onto her subjectivity in a way that students can now see is revealed throughout her narrative; Prince is a strong woman, one who can advocate through her story, and so providing a heroic model of fortitude in the face of extreme suffering.

Equiano has a similar story to tell that usefully compares to Prince's of the rending of the family. Although his begins with his sister's and his abduction by African "slavers," his parents never to be seen again, their strong sibling bond sustains them until the fatal moment when they are broken apart. I ask students to closely compare the two scenes, Prince's and Equiano's, to compare the affective impact of their uses of rhetoric.

> One day … I saw one of those people come into the year of our next neighbor but one, to kidnap, there being many stout young people in it. Immediately on this I gave the alarm … But alas! Ere long it was my fate to be thus attached, and to be carried off, when none of the grown people were nigh … But alas! we were soon deprived of even the small comfort of weeping together … for my sister and I were then separated, while we lay clasped in each other's arms.
>
> (62)

Rhetorically, the "But, alas!" repetition has a lot of work to do, but for a modern reader, it can't carry the weight of the experienced trauma in the way that Prince's "Oh dear! I cannot bear to think of that day,--it is too much.—" still does. If Equiano's response to the loss of his sister is different from Prince's, it strikes the reader as pathos-filled rather than grief-stricken perhaps – so that students try to locate the difference in experienced pain variously – I've found it helpful to shift their attention to seeing that the way the story is told can change the emotional register, and that the way emotion is being put to use should not influence us to value or devalue one person's pain over another's given our historical biases.

In Olaudah Equiano we have a traveler, businessman, and finally English gentleman. In Mary Prince we initially have the helpless victim, much in the vein of Wordsworth's forsaken Indian woman, but she quickly turns heroic in her endurance and spirit, and so she is more like Felicia Hemans's Indian woman raging against the patriarchal conditions, although Prince could not express such anger in her story and so maintains a distanced voice when describing her own pain. Indeed, she presents herself as stoically heroic, her spirit bearing witness to her strength rather than any specific act.

A heroic Black figure whose strength as well as spirit captured the Romantic imagination was a rebel slave whose story was told in William Earle's *Obi or, The History of Three-Fingered Jack* (1800). Although Earle sensationalizes the role of **Obi**, or **Obeah**, an African derived religion similar to voodoo, his Jamaica-based novella is based on the real enslaved rebellions taking place in British colonies. Three-fingered Jack was a historical figure legendary in the Caribbean, but so little is known of him that Earle imagines a backstory for his family that begins in Africa where his parents are betrayed by an English trader they befriend and nurse back to health. The theme of white betrayal of Black characters is a common theme for abolitionist literature, as it sentimentalizes the moral nature of the relationship over the more difficult political aspects. Although it was of course the politics that matter, readers could be won over through sentiment much more easily. Therefore, the romance of both Jack's parents is paramount to understanding why Jack risks his own life to free his fellow enslaved people. In the novel his father is depicted as an outsized heroic figure, almost Samson-like in his strength and courage. From him Jack gains the heroic qualities that make him a rebel leader. Such positive examples of enslaved rebellion, even when they end badly for the hero, were important to the work of the abolitionist cause.

Another, and very real, example of the heroic can be seen in the history of San Domingo (now Haiti) and Toussaint L'Ouverture's extraordinary transformation of the colony into a free state by 1803. The only fully successful rebellion by enslaved peoples, the Haitian Revolution was considered to be fully in keeping with the spirit of the French Revolution and can be considered a historical event of Black Romanticism. Toussaint suffers none of the rending of family that Prince and Equiano experience, and his political acuity and gracious use of political speech acts and his tolerance as a political leader for all San Domingans; his voice and message are clear in quotations from letters and speeches: "Learn, citizens, to appreciate the glory of your new political status. In acquiring the rights that the Constitution accords to all Frenchmen, do not forget the duties it imposes on you. Be but virtuous and you will be French men and good citizens … Work together for the prosperity of San Domingo … [to] assure public well-being" (James 205).

A heroic figure working in the South American territory of the Spanish Empire, bent on bettering the lives of others like Toussaint L'Ouverture, was Simon Bolivar. His achievements, and those who wrote poetry and essays to celebrate them – as well as to dramatize the victimization of indigenous civilizations such as Richard Sheridan's 1799 play *Pizarro*. Adapting a German Romantic play by August von Kotzebue, Sheridan made the heroic Incan response to the Spanish conquest of their empire spectacular. The pageantry of this play-spectacle allowed audiences to imagine themselves into an earlier time and complex civilization, with outsized architecture and foreign landscapes yet with recognizable heroes and heroines. The commemorative works about Bolivar's achievements were no less Romantically pro-revolution, if less vividly presented. Byron's lyric to Bolivar, as well as his mention of the revolutionary in several of his letters – as well as his renaming of his schooner "Bolivar" – testifies to the iconic stature of the man, and it is possible Byron took him for a model when he traveled to Greece to aid the Greek War for Independence. Unlike Toussaint L'Ouverture, for whom poems and artistic representations such as Wordsworth's "To Toussaint L'Ouverture" focused on his betrayal by the French and subsequent martyrdom (the first line of Wordsworth's poem is "Toussaint, the most unhappy of men!"), Bolivar's reception focused on his heroic achievements.

Called "El Libertador" in the South American colonies of the Spanish Empire he led or helped lead to independence what are now Venezuela (his own colony), Colombia, Bolivia, Peru, Ecuador, and Panama. The first war for independence he participated in was that of Venezuela, first attempted by Francisco de Miranda with the aid of American volunteers in 1806, and first realized in 1811, then after initial failure it finally succeeded in 1830. But in the process of fighting on different fronts, Bolivar was exiled several times: in 1815 he escaped to Jamaica, and a year later he sailed to Haiti where he befriended the Haitian revolutionary leader Alexandre Pétion, connecting his work with that of Toussaint's groundbreaking success with the successes Bolivar was to accomplish on his return to South America.

The achievements of Equiano, Prince, and of liberators such as Toussaint and Bolivar – self-improvement, self-liberation, the liberation of a people – participate in the very conditions that fueled the French Revolution, financed by France's slave trade-enriched bourgeoisie,and the English abolition movement. C.L.R. James argues that the latter was encouraged by William Pitt as Prime Minister to deflect other political tensions (53–4).

THE BRIDGE BETWEEN SELF AND OTHER: BLACK ROMANTICISM

Although the most powerful Black voices were raised in the cause of abolition during the period, few works of fiction or poetry that were not overtly political in theme or expressing sympathy for the plight of Black people, such as Blake's "Little Black Boy," focused on their inner lives. An important exception is the anonymous novel *The Woman of Colour,* published in 1808. Its publication date is just two years after three politicians – Wilberforce, Charles Fox, and Lord Milbanke – spent a summer in Parliamentary debates arguing the merits of abolition (most likely the years when the novel was composed), and just a year after the Slave Trade Act was finally passed. It is not the first fictional work to pose a Black person as protagonist, but the one with the most identifiably Black voice and subjectivity, and scholars have argued for the likelihood that the unknown author was also Black or mixed race.

The novel's heroine resembles the difficult legacies of several mixed-race heiresses, whose fathers wanted to control who they married. For example, the wealthy Jamaican plantation owner James Wright, who died in 1806 near London, left a will in which his two illegitimate mixed-race daughters could only inherit if they married in England, where they were living at the time. The implication is that they would have to marry white Englishmen. A more well-known heiress at the time was Dido Elizabeth Belle. The illegitimate daughter of a Royal Navy officer, she was brought as a child to live with his uncle William Murray, 1st Earl of Mansfield (see Poser 286–300). The Murrays educated Belle, raising her at Kenwood House together with another great-niece, Lady Elizabeth Murray; a now famous portrait of the two girls hung at Kenwood House and was likely painted as part of their entrance into the marriage market. In his will of 1793, Lord Mansfield officially freed Belle and provided a small inheritance for her although he did not claim her as his niece. And although she was unrestricted by the will and did marry a white man, he was of the working classes and she was reduced to that social status.

What Belle experienced more than Wright's daughters was the force of patriarchy heightened by racism. In *The Woman of Colour*, however, the critique of patriarchy comes to the fore through the way the inheritance plot unfolds, whereas the critique of enslavement – which the heroine is both the result and beneficiary of – is mediated, since she maintains that there can be beneficent plantation owners, as her loving father was. But patriarchy, as Olivia Fairfield's situation and experiences make clear, is what makes enslavement possible in the first place, since it is patriarchy that proclaims the right of a man to own a woman – his wife, daughter, niece – and to have legal power over even his mother or aunts. It is a small extension for a man to own another man, then, and enslavement is just a more horrific version of serfdom and indentured servitude (one that permits torture and murder to seem commonplace, and although this does not enter into the novel, small cruelties suggest it). Mr. Fairfield did not marry his beautiful enslaved woman, the mother of Oliva, and this is the one act his daughter does not forgive the otherwise (in her eyes) model plantation owner.

The plot of *The Woman of Colour* centers on the heroine's own account of her experiences as she travels to England to marry her white cousin in accordance with her father's will; if she does not, her inheritance will pass to her elder married cousin who will have custody over her. As this man and his wife are both greedy and ambitious, Olivia is aware that marriage to her cousin Augustus is the better choice, but he is oddly hesitant. After their marriage, it is revealed that his sister-in-law has been scheming since before Olivia's arrival to gain control over both Augustus and then Olivia's fortune. Olivia is undone by the discovery that the wife of Augustus's first, secret marriage is still alive, and that their child lives with her; a fact concealed by the sister-in-law, and revealed by her at a precise moment for her plot against the newlyweds. Although the novel is a work of domestic fiction, it contains a strong indictment of patriarchy and enslavement with clear connections between the two. That the villain of the novel is a woman (the sister-in-law), it is also clear that her ambitions are the product of her own disempowerment under patriarchy.

Another critique of patriarchy in the novel is that of the Nabobs, who are part of London society. One couple in particular reveals themselves to be not only vulgar – the typical criticism of these newly wealthy commoners – but that they are cruel as well. Their wealth, coming from the mistreatment of colonial subjects in India, makes them cruel to everyone, but particularly Olivia as a mixed-race woman. She can see how deeply they are marked by patriarchy in the way they are raising their son to be overtly cruel to everyone.

Because it is a work of domestic romance, *The Woman of Colour* participates in one of the most popular literary genres during the Romantic period. It is in line with all of Jane Austen's novels as these engage with patriarchy, but particularly with *Mansfield Park* in which there is also the plantation owner who is not quite the perfect patriarch. But more than the critique of patriarchy, it is the critique of empire, through the horrifying Nabobs, enslavement, and Olivia's spirited defense of her "brothers and sisters" in

Jamaica, that makes the anonymous novel a Romantic work, and more specifically (given the scholarly opinion of the author's race) a Black Romantic work.

BROWN ROMANTICISM

Work is currently being done in the area of what scholar Manu Samriti Chander terms **Brown Romanticism**, in reference to literary production in Southeast Asia during or resulting from the Romantic period. These works, largely written in India, combine aspects of Hindi and Sanskrit epics with Romantic ideas and the Romantic aesthetic. In addition to the hugely popular translations of Sir William Jones, and the English poetry in imitation of them, the production of Romantic works written by Indian poets in the peripheries of the British Empire helps illustrate how powerful the Romantic effect was. And how empire and consumerism could cohabit with Romantic revolutionary thought during the period, whether the poetry of Percy Shelley or the travelogue of Abu Talib Khan or the poetry of one of his countrymen.

SUMMARY

In this chapter, the ways that empire and its reach change life at home and abroad are explored:

- Through Cook's voyages, we see the connection between knowledge acquisition and imperial power.
- Politics, trade, and consumerism were intricately connected: ambassadors served to further trade compacts, objects collected provided the foundations of national museums.
- Crown-supported companies became central to imperial growth; the most important for Europe and Britain were the companies trading in India and the East Indies, such as the East India Company, and its related intellectual component, the Royal Asiatic Society.
- "The Orient" became a prime way to organize East–West relations; "Orientalism" became the key to assimilating Eastern cultures and goods by providing an aesthetic through which

to translate all goods, peoples, and histories of the Middle East and Far East.

- Similarly, the West Indies and Indigenous peoples of North America were aestheticized and assimilated into British culture; similar effects were produced in France and Spain.
- The increasing publication of texts by formerly enslaved peoples produced what is now termed Black Romanticism; similarly, Red Romanticism and Brown Romanticism indicate the literary expression of non-white Romantic writers.

FURTHER READING

For the relation between empire, power, and sex see Colville and Williams's biography of Emma Hamilton, the scandalous wife of Sir William Hamilton. For a closer look at how the colony can make the empire, see Dirks's *The Scandal of Empire: India and the Creation of Imperial Britain*. For the story of Haiti's imporance to France's financial solvency, see Dubois's *Avengers of the New World: The Story of the Haitian Revolution*. For an overview of abolition see Sinha's *The Slave's Cause*. Coleridge's enigmatic poem "Kubla Khan" has a fascinating background; still valuable and enjoyable is Lowes's *The Road to Xanadu*. For a broader perspective, see Roe's *Samuel Taylor Coleridge and the Sciences of Life*. On why people took tinctures of opium, see Adkins's *Eavesdropping on Jane Austen's England*. A good overview of the medicinal uses of laudanum, as well as its literary connections, is McIntosh's blog post "Cure to Craving: Laudanum's Lure in the 18th, 19th, and 20th Centuries." Richard Sheridan's *Pizarro* is well worth reading: the Broadview edition contextualizes the play and provides visuals of the spectacular and innovative staging. Ostergard's catalogue for an exhibition on William Beckford is a visually rich introduction to the materiality of empire.

WEBSITES

Royal Asiatic Society of Great Britain and Ireland. https://royalasiaticsociety.org/.

"Women in History: Dido Belle." *English Heritage*. https://www.english-heritage.org.uk/learn/histories/women-in-history/dido-belle/.

WORKS CITED

Adkins, L., and R. Adkins. *Eavesdropping on Jane Austen's England: How Our Ancestors Lived Two Centuries Ago*. London: Little, Brown, 2013.

Blake, William. "Little Black Boy." In *Songs of Innocence and Experience*. Copy L, 1795. https://www.blakearchive.org/copy/songsie.l?descId=songsie.l.illbk.08.

Chander, Manu Samriti. *Brown Romantics: Poetry and Nationalism in the Global Nineteenth Century*. Lewisburg: Bucknell University Press, 2017.

Colville, Quintin, and Kate Williams. *Emma Hamilton: Seduction and Celebrity*. London: Thames & Hudson, 2016.

Daut, Marlene. *Baron de Vastey and the Origins of Black Atlantic Humanism*. New York: Palgrave Macmillan, 2017.

De Quincey, Thomas. *Confessions of an English Opium-Eater*. Edited by Joel Faflak. Peterborough: Broadview, 2009.

Dirks, Nicholas. *The Scandal of Empire: India and the Creation of Imperial Britain*. Cambridge: Harvard University Press, 2006.

Dubois, Laurent. *Avengers of the New World: The Story of the Haitian Revolution*. Cambridge: Harvard University Press, 2004.

Earle, William. *Obi or, The History of Three-Fingered Jack*. Edited by Srinivas Aravamudan. Peterborough: Broadview Press, 2005.

Equiano, Olaudah. *The Interesting Narrative of the Life of Olaudah Equiano*. London: Simon & Brown, 1789.

Fulford, Tim. *Romantic Indians: Native Americans, British Literature, and Transatlantic Culture 1756–1830*. Oxford: Oxford University Press, 2006.

Hemans, Felicia. "Indian Woman's Death Song." In *Records of Woman: With Other Poems*, 103–8. Edinburgh: John Johnston, 1828.

Holmes, Richard. *Coleridge: Early Visions, 1772–1804*. New York: Pantheon, 1989.

James, C. L. R. *The Black Jacobins*. London: Allison & Busby, 1980.

Khan, Abu Talib. *The Travels of Mirza Abu Taleb Khan*. Edited by Daniel O'Quinn. Peterborough: Broadview, 2008.

Lowes, John. *The Road to Xanadu: A Study in the Ways of the Imagination*. New York: Houghton Mifflin, 1927.

McIntosh, Matthew A. "Cure to Craving: Laudanum's Lure in the 18th, 19th, and 20th Centuries," June 4, 2025. https://brewminate.com/cure-to-craving-laudanums-lure-in-the-18th-19th-and-20th-centuries/.

Ostergard, Derek E., ed. *William Beckford 1760–1844: An Eye for the Magnificent*. New Haven: Yale University Press, 2001.

Patterson, Jessica. "William Jones and the Study of Hinduism." *Global Intellectual History* 10, no. 2 (2025): 109–17.

Poser, Norman S. *Lord Mansfield: Justice in the Age of Reason*. Montreal: McGill-Queen's University Press, 2013.

Prince, Mary. *The History of Mary Prince, a West Indian Slave by Mary Prince*, 1831. https://www.maryprince.org/the-slave-narrative.

Roe, Nicholas. *Samuel Taylor Coleridge and the Sciences of Life*. Oxford: Oxford University Press, 2001.

Sheridan, Richard. *Pizarro*. Edited by Selena Couture and Alexander Dick. Peterborough: Broadview, 2017.

Sinha, Manisha. *The Slave's Cause: A History of Abolition*. New Haven: Yale University Press, 2017.

Wordsworth, William. "Complaint of a Forsaken Indian Woman." In *Lyrical Ballads*, edited by W. Wordsworth and S. T. Coleridge, 191–6. London: J. & A. Arch, 1798.

3

GENDER COMPLEXITIES, GENDER EXPRESSION

INTRODUCTION

How did Romantic period writers depict gender identity and relations between differently gendered people? For one thing, the shift from 18th-century societal norms to Victorian ones which occurred during the period reveals how gender norms were beginning to formulate in a modernist schema although the period remained fluid almost until the late 1830s. The 18th century emphasized appearance, to some degree continuing the medieval sartorial regulations that identified a person by their dress, as in the forester's tunic, leggings, and cap we recognize as the Robin Hood costume. But change was underway, and early in the century dress indicated class and wealth more than profession. Whereas 18th-century middling classes emphasized a woman's natural femininity over the artifices of court life, Romantic period mothers tended to spend large sums on their daughters' ball dresses when they came of age to enhance their appearance, even to seem of a wealthier family. It was less what you were born into than what you could become; your potential was now an important factor as you entered society.

It is that social fluidity that allowed writers freer exploration of characters' behavior, psychology, and individuality, which in turn diluted some of the rigid conventions concerning heroic protagonists and beautiful but passive heroines inherited from medieval romance. This freer exploration was already in evidence with the

DOI: 10.4324/9781032625744-4

18th-century **rise of the novel**: Samuel Richardson's *Clarissa* (1748) exemplifies the passive heroine who finds her agency through resistance and perseverance. We can see these traits in Jane Austen's **doubled heroine** of *Pride and Prejudice* (1813): Jane Bennet's character is passive but her strength lies in her endurance, while Elizabeth is more independent, defending herself against two poorly motivated marriage proposals and, staged as a battle royale, against the powerful Lady Catherine de Bourgh. Her agency is what captivates the hero Mr. Darcy before he understands how that agency changes the relational dynamic. His suspension of judgment of Elizabeth's personality depicts a new conception of character: it was now understood to be dynamic rather than static, or at least people worth knowing were changeable while those who refused to change despite circumstances or interlocutors were not. Elizabeth Bennet is worth knowing; her mother is not. Although Jane Bennet's character seems less changeable, the suffering she endures makes her stronger and is also in stark contrast to her mother, who refuses to cope with any kind of stress or threat.

WHAT IS "NORMAL"?

If less rigid norms concerning male and female identity, and to some extent social rank identity, mark the Romantic period, it was not simply a matter of the revolutionary ideas arising in hot debates concerning political justice stemming from the French Revolution. It was also due to cultural shifts caused by increased industrialism and consumerism (more clothes, books, and other commodities were available at an increasing rate and more affordably) and to increased global trade, which brought other cultures and their histories into view. If this period also saw the shift to nationalism and patriotism, so that Britain seemed the epitome of a civilized polity, people could now see (through the lenses of travel writing or exhibitions) how men and women in other cultures lived and behaved. It was increasingly possible to imagine other ways of being in the world, even of different kinds of gendered dress, and if this was a lesser influence than imported commodities, it did free up conceptions of gender identity.

Moreover, romanticism allowed for a freer literary exploration of the question of desire, and of queer desire largely constructed (that is, along a gender continuum rather than only hetero male, hetero female, gay, or bisexual). Victorian disciplining of sexual identity had not yet taken place, and the Romantic period saw overt and more hidden sexual modalities and relationships, including *menage a trois*, "free love," "romantic friendship" (a lesbian relationship culturally interpreted as non-sexual even when it wasn't), "Sapphic" sexual relations ("criminal" lesbianism), accepted (covert) and criminalized (outed) homosexuality and bisexuality, as well as non-binary identity, and more fluid identities. Queer reading practices and queer theory can tease out sexual play in canonical and non-canonical British romantic texts that may have formerly seemed conventional, and it can make sense of aspects of texts that are queerish – that is, open to queer reading. Queerness has everything to do with gender identity in this period because ideas about gender were shifting. Ultimately, they would land hard on strict bi-morphic templates for what constitutes the male and the female in the Victorian period, but these conventional ideas were being challenged by more liberal ideas of sexuality and gender expression, often simply in how people chose to live their lives.

One of the most visible representations of Romantic period gender expression is the **dandy**. In a fashionable lineage that includes the "macaroni" (young men who dieted to become slender and wore Italian outfits with exaggerated hats that feminized their bodies), the dandy was a signal figure of Romantic period culture. The dandy's outfit and behavior during the Regency (1811–1820) were heavily influenced by the socially ambitious Beau Brummell, the middle-class younger son of the private secretary to Lord North, the Prime Minister, who rose through sheer personality to become a friend of the Prince of Wales. The very model of the dandy, Brummell devised an outfit composed of buck-colored, skin-tight trousers tucked into knee-high boots, a tightly fitted dark blue coat, a top hat and cane, and his signature touch, a highly starched pure white elaborate cravat that took, by his own account, hours for his valet to knot to his satisfaction. The dandy was recognized both by his obsession over dress and his feminized airs. Brummell's success in this role made him one of the most important arbiters of fashion and social influencers during the Regency.

Because of the dandy's intentional blurring of gender expression, which had no relation to sexual desire – dandies could be heteronormative as well as gay with no visible distinguishing mark between the two – gender fluidity was a fashionable mode. Young bucks could behave in aggressively masculine or homosocially fluid ways, and young lovers could affect effeminate behavior to court young women. The dandy's self-conscious posturing and witty aphorisms were gender play at its most visible. But it was the prerogative of male-assigned bodies; women had to discover other ways to escape the limitations of sexual norms, discussed later.

Another part of the shifting ideas about gender had to do with the hot debate on women's rights in the radical years of the 1790s: women writers such as Mary Hays and, more famously, Mary Wollstonecraft, discussed and wrote on their views concerning the human and individual rights women are entitled to. It was a debate that in the second half of the 1790s seemed to be stoppered by both an increasingly conservative reaction in governmental and societal circles to the French Revolutionary threat to British sovereignty and to intentionally misogynistic publications along the lines of Richard Polwhele's *The Unsex'd Females* (1798). It was no help that unintentionally misogynistic publications of liberal philosophers like William Godwin, husband of Wollstonecraft, laid blame on a woman's radical sexual beliefs and behavior. Godwin's revelations in his *Memoirs of the Author of a Vindication of the Rights of Woman* (1798), written a year after her death, whether witting or unwitting, publicly defamed her and consequently diminished the enormous contributions of her feminist and political justice publications. Mary Robinson's *A Letter to the Women of England* (1799) soon followed to correct some of the damage to the reputations of women philosophers and writers – Wollstonecraft is heavy on her mind in this late essay – while its lateness helps contextualize the 1790s human rights debate in relation to gender identity. But the period which followed also debated, as Freud famously put it, "What do women want?" – that is, how to understand women's desire. Female desire and women's rights were inextricably bound; Wollstonecraft makes this clear in her *Vindication of the Rights of Woman* (1792) by focusing on how education can turn women's attention away from "coquetry" (flirting) as the only form of power available to them and toward more socially productive uses of their talents and intelligence. Sexual relations, she suggests, have been reduced to a mere game of flirtation and assignations, a game that was draining the bourgeois domestic space of its lifeblood in imitation of the aristocracy who, in her view, had already gone that path.

Despite Wollstonecraft's efforts to turn the tide on how women's sexuality was viewed, fiction and poetry from the 1790s through the 1820s frequently questioned how sex and gender may be separate from the bodies we are born into, whether by focusing on effeminate male characters and overly domineering women who assume male privilege, or by expressing queer (non-normative hetero) desire or codes so that readers can find what they want in them. These writerly preoccupations closely tracked real social behaviors, interests, concerns, and gossip, to represent life as it was being lived and experienced in ways that subsequent readers have historically failed to recognize until more recent decades. For instance, Jane Austen's *Pride and Prejudice* (1813) uses the stereotype of the effeminate man (Mr. Collins) and the domineering woman (Lady Catherine de Bourgh) to great comic effect, but her doing so not only provides important contrast to the less flashy or fashionable masculinity of Mr. Darcy (the flashy portrayed by Mr. Wickham; the fashionable by Mr. Bingley), but also the non-traditional femininity of Elizabeth Bennet. The battle of power that Lady Catherine engages Elizabeth in ends with the victory of quick wit and intelligence over Lady Catherine's aristocratic (and fairly masculine) privilege. Additionally, Austen shows that gender is a matter of education. Lydia Bennet did not receive the same tutoring and cultural broadening as her two eldest sisters Jane and Elizabeth; Mr. Collins attended university but did not absorb either the intellectual or social experiences a university education should confer. Both characters act out in ways deemed incorrect for their gender.

More overtly, the more politically radical Robinson addresses the question of whether gender is biological or taught in *Walsingham, or The Pupil of Nature* (1797). The protagonist of that novel is emasculated at every turn while his cousin, Sir Sidney Aubrey, whom he deems his antagonist, is revealed in the dénouement to be a young woman educated to behave and even fence like a man. The education is so successful that her disguise fools everyone (even her intensely feminine friend learns of it only because Sidney confides in her); what undoes Sidney, forcing her to reveal her secret, is her own confusion over sexual identity. In love with Walsingham, she could only torment him when playing the man, but as a woman she could both win him over and restore to him his fortune. Her sexual desire, in other words, determines her future, and that desire is biologically based. That Robinson ends the controversial questions her novel raises by resorting to biological destiny – Sidney can never be happy, the narrative makes clear, until she can appear and behave as a woman who desires – is complicated by the fact that Walsingham's advisor and former tutor declares that Sidney must be reeducated to "become" feminine. This is the very tutor who taught Walsingham to behave in a manly way, heroically but with humility. This is in direct contrast to the aristocratic privilege of other male characters who are portrayed as bullies, cheats, liars, and cowards because their rank has destroyed both their individual and civic virtue. For Robinson and Austen both, sex is biologically stable whereas gender is not natural but must be taught – if not at birth, then certainly by the time of late childhood, a concept Freud will later also hold to be true. Boys and girls must learn to behave as chivalrous knights and ladies, but the lessons learned can easily be the wrong ones, so that boys become bullies and predators instead of honorable knights, and girls become manipulative and power-seeking instead of genteel ladies. Moreover, this education does not determine sexual preference.

Indeed, the times and its literature were both rife with the discomfort and frustration of individuals with too-tightly defined gender positions. Extraordinary women like the queer, possibly trans, diarist Anne Lister were not unique individuals to be set aside along with Sappho of Ancient Lesbos and other icons of lesbian and queer achievement. More people were expressing their gender fluidly than we have records of, but the archival evidence shows that trans and queer experience was not as isolated as we might think (Heyman 3–7). More prominently, we have the history of the Chevalier d'Éon, a transwoman of extraordinary courage and martial skill, singular only because she persuaded the King of France to have her legally recognized as a woman and was publicly known to be a transvestite – engaging in fencing spectacles in her voluminous female dress against less encumbered male opponents (Brogan 87–8). Whereas in *Walsingham* transvestism is forced on Sidney by her scheming mother to ensure an inheritance, d'Éon embraces cross-dressing in order to live her life more freely. Anne Lister, living toward the end of the Romantic period, does not dress as a man but her journal entries as a young woman chronicle continuous efforts to tailor and redesign her items of clothing to help her feel more masculine: a kind of coming out in code, as it were. The women in her local community during this period were fascinated by her masculine behavior and conversation, and engaged in gossip both with and without her concerning whether she will make some young woman her conquest. And she is enormously interested by their gossip, half willing to educate them to a broader conception of their personal freedom and half concerned to control the conversation to keep it from getting too dangerous for her.

The popular imagination about lesbian love, however, was confined to "female friendship," made popular by the Ladies of Llangollen, who had by this time become famous as romantic friends and intellectuals living contentedly together in Wales, visited by celebrities and tourists alike (Vicinus 9). What Lister chronicles in her journals, however, is the reality underlying the cultural fiction of women's "romantic" friendships: there she is frank about her sexual desire, her exploits, and her obsessions. Lister kept these sections of her journal entries and her most explicit letters in a code that only her most trusted lovers could read, which illustrates how dangerous to reputation and even life the reality of queer love could be. People of rank were treated differently, often having to go into exile, whereas men of lesser rank caught in homosexual acts could be publicly humiliated and hanged, as sodomy was a capital offense. But Wollstonecraft points out in the *Vindication*, unregulated sexuality regardless of one's gender and whether queer or heteronormative was problematic, destructive to society, and dangerous. Perhaps one of the best examples of how not everyone shared this view of promiscuity was Lord Byron, who was only the more attractive for becoming labeled by his erstwhile lover Lady Caroline Lamb as "mad, bad, and dangerous to know." Secretly bisexual, Byron enjoyed having Lamb dress as a page for their assignations; in addition to the titillation this afforded both of them, it also created a cover for visits from adolescent boys (Crompton 197–8, 200).

GENDER FLUIDITY AND GENDER NORMS

The "free love" movement of the radical 1790s involved love triangles where married and unmarried persons expanded the aristocratic practice of arranged marriages and tolerated mistresses and lovers within the marital arrangement. Mary Wollstonecraft believed in its liberating potential and attempted to form a free love relationship with the Swiss painter Henri Fuseli and his wife, who did not appreciate this radicalization of her marriage (St. Clair 182–5). One way to understand what radicals were attempting in revising or debunking the marriage institution was to break open institutions that bound people to lives they didn't want. William Blake called this the "mind-forged manacles" of contemporary life, since institutions are only as powerful as people's combined complicity in following regulations and laws whether just or not.

Another way to think of it is as polyamory, a concept that has gained traction in our own cultural moment. Polyamory allows for friendship connections to mix with sexual relations, and some argue it signals a current need for more friendship generally in our lives. That free love and women's "romantic friendships" coexisted in the same period indicates that the Romantic period was strongly inclined to consider the French motto of "liberty, equality, and brotherhood" to indicate a liberation from parental and monarchical constraints and an increased valuing of friends (brothers) over family. Although family remained important, this attitude did loosen up how regimented parents could be over their children's – particularly their daughters' – behavior. That this loosening accompanied the rising acceptance, at least in literary works, of romantic love over contract marriages indicates that the fluidity of thinking about sex and gender was extending to how people could imagine their lives. For instance, when

Henry Austen, one of Jane Austen's favorite older brothers, married their widowed cousin Eliza de Feuillide, it was a love match but also tremendously romantic since her first husband, the Count de Feuillide, had been beheaded in the French Reign of Terror only a couple of years after their marriage in Paris. And Percy Bysshe Shelley, already married to Harriet Westbrook and father of two, eloped to the continent with Mary Godwin in 1814, living a "free love" relationship until Harriet's suicide two years later enabled them to marry (St. Clair 351–5). Like Eliza Austen, the romance of Mary Godwin's unconventional relation was more in the imagination than the harsh realities of revolution in the first case and exile in the second, but both examples indicate that romantic love was gaining ascendancy in real life as well. And it must be noted that Percy Shelley's attitude toward love was polyamorous, and Mary Shelley had to put up with his relations with other women in their marriage. Free love and romantic friendship, and to an extent polyamory, mix eros (sexual love) and agape (self-sacrificing love). It is this mixture that Romantic era writers were attracted to, but thinkers like Samuel Taylor Coleridge were pondering a more basic boundary.

In his notebooks he wrote:

> There is a period in a man's life, varying in various men, from thirty-five to forty-five, and operating most strongly in bachelors, widowers, or those worst and miserablest widowers, unhappy husbands, in which a man finds himself at the *top of the hill*, and having attained, perhaps, what he wishes, begins to ask himself, What is all this for?—begins to feel the vanity of his pursuits, becomes half-melancholy, gives in to wild dissipation or self-regardless drinking; and some, not content with these (not *slow*) poisons, destroy themselves, and leave their ingenious female or female-minded friends to fish out some *motive*.
>
> (*Anima Poetae* 196)

Masculinity loses its power when its motives are called into question, and most particularly when it gives in to the small-mindedness of women friends or of "female-minded" male companions. Although Coleridge is thinking about gender identity here instead of sexual desire or Platonic love, what this memorandum suggests is that sexual desire was still pitted against gender stereotyping even though Romantic-period individuals experienced greater freedom in gender expression than later when Freud was crystallizing his theories. "I had *felt* this truth, but never saw it before clearly: it came upon me at Malta under the melancholy, dreadful feeling of finding myself to be *man*, by a distinct division from boyhood, youth, and 'young man,'" Coleridge writes, emphasizing the moment a man questions his status as one that to some extent effeminizes him: "Dreadful was the feeling" (197).

What Freud theorized concerning sexual identity was predicated on concepts of the child already at work in the Romantic period. As he worked to differentiate "libidinal types" (the erotic, the narcissistic, and the obsessional), Freud relied on his theory of infant libidinal experience in "Some Psychical Consequences of The Anatomical Distinction Between the Sexes" (1925). Here, he asserts that the infant has an active libido that cathects to different objects such as the mother's breast and the baby's own thumb, but not to the genital region until later in childhood. This sense of the child's uncrystallized sexuality was dominant in Romantic period thinking, allowing parents to account for tomboyish behavior among girls and more passive pursuits among boys without undue concern. Indeed, a boy was not dressed in breeches before between two and eight years old: he was "unbreeched," all children wearing a gown until this acknowledgment of gender difference took place. In other words, anatomical difference and gender did not automatically align; gender, as Austen's and Robinson's novels demonstrate, is not inherent but must be taught. Freud agreed: for him, gender is taken on by the child during the Oedipal Crisis where boys learn to adopt their father's masculine behaviors whereas girls begin to flirt with their father to win his attention. The difference lies in the Romantic period's openness to different expressions of gender, whereas for Freud the Victorian prejudices concerning variant expressions meant that he viewed difference as pathological: non-submissive women were hysterical (as in his famous case study of "Dora") while homosexuals were perverse.

Moreover, the ungendered child was newly conceived in the late 1780s and 1790s as the "**romantic child**." This was a conception of the child that broke with traditional understandings of children as little adults waiting to grow up; instead, the child carried with them the innocence but also the spiritual connection of the soul before it is born into a body. This childlike innocence allowed for an immediate connection to nature, which later they would have to unlearn to enter the adult world. "**Nature poets**" like Wordsworth and Coleridge embraced this vision of the child, although Coleridge was more liable to think of young children as ungendered. Wordsworth's "Ode, Intimations of Immortality" (1807) features the child as marked by "he," possibly because it is a self-reference ("The Child is father of the Man" is the poem's first line) since his daughter Catherine was also considered by the family and friends to be the perfect example of the romantic child. Wordsworth's depiction differs from William Blake's in *Songs of Innocence and Experience* (1794) in which different poems portray children in one of the two states not because they have moved from childish innocence to the suffering experience causes, but because these are two states of the soul that Blake believed we move back and forth between whether child or adult. In Wordsworth's Intimations Ode, the child more straightforwardly progresses from the newborn's trailing of heavenly existence (the soul's state before entering a body) to increasing experience of human trials and suffering.

> Thou little Child, yet glorious in the might
> Of heaven-born freedom on thy being's height,
> Why with such earnest pains dost thou provoke
> The years to bring the inevitable yoke,
> Thus blindly with thy blessedness at strife?
> Full soon thy Soul shall have her earthly freight.
>
> *(VIII, 122–7)*

This less complex vision of the romantic child, as having the innate purity and sanctity of the divinely touched, is not only an idealized image of early childhood; it also contains a strong dose of nostalgia, a suggestion of the adult yearning for his own earlier days when things were simple and full of joy rather than despair. Coleridge echoes this view of childhood in a letter:

> The wisdom and graciousness of God in the infancy of the human species—its beauty, long continuance, etc. (Children in the wind—hair floating, tossing, a miniature of the agitated trees below which

> they played. The elder whirling for joy the one in petticoats, a fat baby eddying half-willingly, half by the force of the gust, driven backward, struggling forward—both drunk with the pleasure, both shouting their hymn of joy.)
>
> (*Letters*, 408)

Whereas Coleridge writes about children as nongendered, in Wordsworth's masterful ode both child and the adult speaker are male. Moreover, there is no suggestion that the child's soul is feminine – the traditional gendering of the soul in a male body. However, when Thomas De Quincey captures his love for Catherine Wordsworth, who died at age five, in his *Confessions of an English Opium-Eater* (1821), she is portrayed as the very emblem of the romantic child. Both she and Ann, the young prostitute who befriended De Quincey when, a penniless stranger, he first came to London and who also died young, are rendered in the *Confessions* as ideals of feminine purity. It is the innocence of their spirits that he celebrates in mourning their early deaths, but the way he presents his visions of them, which he experiences as positive versions of his opium dreams, effectively embalms both Catherine and Ann within his memoirs. Held in his nostalgia and visions, they are not real people; they are embodied female souls, making them unfit for the harshness of real life. (By contrast, self-possessed or productive women were often admired for their "masculine" spirit.) But they are not treated equally: Catherine's innocence is in stark contrast with the suffering Ann endured, although De Quincey suggests without irony that his difficulties were of the same nature as hers: "Successors too many, to myself and Ann, have doubtless since then trodden in our footsteps, inheritors of our calamities; other orphans than Ann have sighed; tears have been shed by other children" (81). Here De Quincey agrees with Blake that experience disregards gender, but innocence – particularly in the sense of the romantic child – seems for him to belong to the female.

Mary Shelley's novella *Mathilda* (c. 1819–1820) is in a vein of women's writing, such as Mary Hays's *Victim of Prejudice*, that counters the idea that the destruction of childish innocence is ungendered, although it doesn't contest the desirability and nostalgia for that innocence. More specifically, it contests the kind of embalming of the child's purity in adult femininity such as De Quincey's hallucinated visions celebrate. (This idealization of the feminine becomes a characteristic trait of the Victorian imaginary, reaching new heights in Charles Dickens's novels.)

In *Mathilda*, Shelley's heroine is now an adult but has had a painful childhood that has led to her solitary existence and existential crisis. It was a radical work at the time, and resembles her mother's last novel *Maria, or The Wrongs of Woman* (1798) in that the ending suggests the heroine's suicide. But *Mathilda* was even more radical than Wollstonecraft's *Maria* in suggesting the heroine has been molested by her father. Both suicide and incest were taboo subjects, and to put both into one work was unthinkable. These are, however, very real threats to women's lives; the number of women who attempted or successfully ended their lives in London by jumping into the Thames or Hampstead Heath's pond from destitution or other threats was high. While Shelley's depiction of incest and suicide was radical, she was careful to portray her heroine as passive and a victim, making her all the more feminine. But Hays's much earlier depiction of a young woman driven to extremes in *Victim of Prejudice* refused such gender typing, and her heroine, though continually trapped by circumstances and misfortunes, retains her strong sense of agency. This protagonist's strength of character makes her an atypical woman but does not erase her female status. Comparing the two heroines allows us to see how gender was moving closer to the stereotyping that so restricted individual expression in the rest of the 19th century.

Although the psychoanalytic and feminist work of the mid- to late-20th century accomplished much to return gender to a more nuanced understanding, Judith Butler's groundbreaking work *Gender Trouble* (1999) complicated even more how gender was being understood. There Butler draws on Michel Foucault's insight in *The History of Sexuality* that "sex" is a fiction, one that reduces the complexities of human physiology and psychology into a bifurcated scheme of male and female, limiting identities that – particularly since the modernism Foucault identifies as beginning after the French Revolution – one has to fit into. Butler argues that gender is also not a stable term; moreover, it is performative rather than inherent. It is not just *not* inherent, it is also fluid – a conception that aligns well with the new flexibility those in the Romantic period were exploring in gender expression and sexual relations. What Butler's study helps highlight is an aspect of Romantic period life that otherwise goes unnoticed: that sexual activity and sexual identity are not the same thing. Although Michel Foucault had already argued this in the first volume of his *History of Sexuality* (1978) as a demarcation between the medieval and the modern, Butler's detailed argument lays out just how fully the Victorian equation of behavior and identity reduced and constricted individual expression. In 18th-century society, a man who committed sodomy was not a "homosexual" but rather a man who committed criminal acts; it was his choice to do so, and it was his acts that were targeted rather than his identity. Similarly, a woman who dressed as a man and assumed a male persona and identity – often to "marry" another woman – in other words, someone we would recognize today as a trans man, was known as a "**female husband**." This term, like "sodomy," could not be applied to individuals without grave consequences for them; unlike "romantic friendship," "female husband" was understood to be transgressive, but like sodomy, it was also understood to exist. Sexual identity, in other words, was also in some way performative in that individuals not only acted out their sense of their own gender (as in the term already in use of the "masculine woman") but acted on their sexual desire, particularly in the case of bisexuals. Indeed, the aristocratic practice of taking a lover outside the arranged marriage provided the wealthy classes with a cover for bisexual relationships, since the identity of the lover could be hidden.

Another aspect of 20th-century thought on gender and sexuality that is relevant to Romantic period life is the French feminist contributions to understanding heterosexual norms and conventions as artificial. Luce Irigaray (*Speculum of the Other Woman*, 1974) and Monique Wittig (*The Straight Mind, and Other Essays*, 1992) particularly opened up avenues of thought that challenged these conventions on philosophical grounds and speculated on how to express female desire in a language that seems inadequate to that experience. Although the specific challenge they were addressing was in large part Freud's question, "What does woman want?"

their work, too, is relevant to Romantic writing. Their questioning about whether the male should be the model for all things resonates with Romantic conceptions of children, both in the sense of unassigned gender during infancy and early childhood, and in the sense of the romantic child. Irigaray and Wittig's speculations echo Romantic women writers who argue that gendering functions more as a convenient way for part of the population to deprive another part of their human rights.

Mary Robinson's *Letter to the Women of England* is not just an attempt to restore Wollstonecraft's reputation and to revive feminist debates. Godwin's ruinous memoir of Wollstonecraft, as well as misogynist diatribes against her, appeared in 1798. Robinson clearly felt compelled to turn the tide of what appeared to be an increasing consensus that the early 1790s radicalism, with its implications for women's rights, was at an end. It was also a lucid argument for nongendered treatment under the law. As Robinson pointedly makes clear, men have the legal ability to defend their reputations and honor, but women do not. Drawing on the model of chivalry, she argues that women have the same right as men to self-defense.

> Supposing that destiny, or interest, or chance, or what you will, has united a man, confessedly of a weak understanding, and corporeal debility, to a woman strong in all the powers of intellect, and capable of bearing the fatigues of busy life: is it not degrading to humanity that such a woman should be the passive, the obedient slave, of such an husband? Is it not repugnant to all the laws of nature, that her feelings, actions, and opinions, should be controuled, perverted, and debased, by such an help-mate? Can she look for protection to a being ... Impossible, yet, if from prudence, or from pity, if for the security of worldly interest, or worldly happiness, she presumes to take a lead in domestic arrangements, or to screen her wedded shadow from obloquy or ruin, what is she considered by the imperious sex? but an usurper of her husband's rights; a domestic tyrant; a vindictive shrew; a petticoat philosopher; and a disgrace to that race of mortals, known by the degrading appellation of the defenceless sex.
>
> (3–4)

Despite softening this critique of patriarchy in her novels, here Robinson is explicit in her appeal to women to recognize their individual self-expression rather than accept the limitations gendering enforces: "The barbarity of custom's law in this enlightened country, has long been exercised to the prejudice of woman, even the laws of honour have been perverted to oppress her," she adds (5). Robinson makes it clear that there is nothing appealing about femininity if it elevates passivity and victimization over taking charge of "domestic arrangements." She herself did so much more, beginning her writing career while living with her husband and infant in debtor's prison, where he had been placed. She continued to support herself and her daughter by writing throughout a tumultuous and very public life; although frequently associated with the demi-monde, the *Letter* makes clear that earning her livelihood was a virtuous act committed in the face of a dissolute and unaffectionate husband.

But how different is what Robinson argues for from the lives of individuals leading transgressive lives during the period? Like Wollstonecraft, Robinson's manifesto is aimed at the wealthier classes, the "genteel" and those who take advantage of them. But others of various classes were taking their lives into their own hands and quietly performing revolutionary acts of gender expression that were as brave as those she describes in the *Letter.* Some were even more courageous, discussed at the end of the next section.

QUEER ROMANTICISMS

Two now relatively well-known Romantic period women who lived out their sexual identity and gender expression on their own terms were Mary Diana Dods and Anne Lister. The Scottish-born Dods, having moved to London with her sister, became intimate with Mary Shelley and her literary circle. With Mary Shelley's help, Dods was able to live as a trans man and female husband, Walter Sholto Douglas. Dods/Douglas supported himself, his wife, and her child through writing, using the pen name David Lyndsay, the name of a famous 17th-century Scots poet, Sir David Lyndsay (Ewan 102). A fascinating character, Walter Sholto Douglas exemplifies successful gender fluidity. At his death, his daughter (his wife's infant whom he had raised as his own) had no suspicion that he was not her father nor a man. (His name was on her birth certificate.) Douglas's own relations with his Scottish father were tenuous. Both he and his sister were the illegitimate children of George Douglas, the 16th Earl of Morton, who refused to recognize them legally or to support them sufficiently, so that both had to find ways to supplement his gifts. Interestingly, Dods chose to adopt his father's name when transitioning to his new identity, and occasionally emphasized his Scottish roots in his writings, as when he dedicated his short story collection *Tales of the Wild and Wonderful* (published anonymously in 1825 with the aid of Mary Shelley) to Joanna Baillie, the best-known Scots woman writer of the period. As David Lyndsay, Dods/Douglas published dramas and stories in *Blackwood's Magazine*, where previously he had been writing anonymous or signed reviews. Then, at Blackwood's invitation, Dods/Douglas wrote *Dramas of the Ancient World* (1822) with "David Lyndsay" on the title page, indicating that he was now a recognized author (Ewan 102). It is unclear why the *Tales* appeared anonymously three years later, but the very title was sure to draw readership.

Anne Lister, who lived in the last part of the Romantic period and on into the Victorian, has more recently become recognized as a major diarist. It has taken scholars some time to decipher the coded sections of Lister's journals where she kept her most private thoughts relating to sexual desire and activity. In one of her earliest journals, she records her impressions of a woman that everyone recognizes as "masculine," and it becomes clear that she delights in this unrestrained gender expression:

> She is called Frank Pickford. She frightens Emma & seems to enjoy doing so. Miss Pickford is certainly like a gentlewoman & clever, to neither of which can Emma, or the people here, lay claim. Miss Pickford's friend, Miss Threlfall, has West India property. It was 5 or 6, or about 5 hundred a year, but has fallen to almost nothing.
>
> (255–6)

In this entry is both a confiding of how much the gender normative Emma, who nonetheless is greatly curious about Lister's life and sexual preferences, is frightened by a more transgressive gender performance. A day or two later Lister writes: "Got to the lecture room at 12.10 by the old church … Sat next to Miss Pickford as usual … How I can still run after the ladies!" (258). Several entries later Lister records that although she believes she is chasing Miss Pickford, when they walk out Miss Pickford assumes the masculine position, taking Lister's arm and placing herself on the street-side (men walked on this side to protect women from being splashed with mud by passing carriages). Later Lister describes with satisfaction how she turns the tables after several days and takes the gentleman's place herself as they walk.

Another day, having attended the local lecture hall together, Lister offers Miss Pickford a ride home in her newly purchased gig which she drives herself. Responding to something the lecturer had said,

> Miss Pickford spoke of the moon being made masculine by some nations, for instance, by the Germans. I smiled & said the moon had tried both sexes, like old Tiresias, I but that one could not make such an observation to every one. Of course she remembered the story? She said yes. I am not quite certain, tho', whether she did or not. 'Tis not everyone who would (vid. Ovid Meta-morphoses). This led us to talk of saying just what came uppermost, sure that one's meaning would always be properly taken. She held out her hand to shake hands. I set her down at Mrs. Wilcock's gate & we parted very good friends.
>
> (257)

Their discussion, resulting from the lecture by a man who assumed the moon is female, led these two unconventional individuals into a mutual understanding, by Lister's reckoning, of a shared meaning that "would always be properly taken." That sharing was possible because of their equally shared nonconforming gender expression. What is also interesting in these entries is how the word "friend" stands in for a relation that includes participation in a shared sexual desire: Miss Pickford's "friend" is her companion and lover Miss Threlfall (whose inheritance comes from a Caribbean plantation, connecting her globally to the empire), whereas Lister's inheritance is entirely local, centered in gentry landownership. Moreover, Lister considers her conquest of Miss Pickford to consist of being "very good friends" by virtue of the shared understanding of their nonnormative gender expression. This use of friendship connections to broaden circles of safe relationships is a variation on the revolutionary ideal of brotherhood to create safe political circles outside the patriarchal family. Lister is using "friendship" to create, in today's parlance, her "chosen family," a circle of friends and acquaintances that supplements, and largely substitutes for, her biological family.

Although Lister has doubts about her own physicality – she refers several times to her odd body in terms of tailoring her clothes or having them made to make her look less feminine – she had no doubts about her ability to successfully chase and woo other women. She recalls that even in her school days she had a strong record of success this way. What this and her other descriptions of successful wooing suggest is that girls and women in the period were open to lesbian relationships, far more so than had been thought. Although it has been long known that boys were introduced to homosexual activity in boarding schools, the military and navy, and other male-only spheres, and that girls were encouraged to have "particular friends" so that they could experience emotional bonding with another person, it was not known to what extent girls also experimented with lesbian sexuality as boys did (or were forced to) with homosexuality. Lister's journals offer a clear window into this hidden world of gender expression.

Yet, Lister was also ambivalent about her body, as shown by the many entries on tailoring her clothes to suit her idea of herself. That ambivalence can be better understood through the recent theorization of monstrosity as a way of taking control of gender expression. What society considers monstrous can be reappropriated as self-expression; Lister finally comes to a successful design of her habitual dress, which is all black to signal the masculine aspect of her personality, as do the de-feminized parts of the outfit. She is like a Beau Brummell in reverse: where he, the quintessential dandy, feminizes his dress and bodily posture, she masculinizes her dress and bearing. But Brummell became a fashion icon through his self-transformation, whereas Lister was an oddity in her community. To what extent does the eccentricity of her lifestyle, often assuming masculine privilege and behavior such as purchasing a horse and gig, and driving it herself, make her the community's resident oddball? The unusual, the oddity, were analogized with the "monstrous" in 18th-century thought. The "monster" is that which is beyond category, as in Mary Shelley's

Frankenstein creature. Lister monster-izes herself in order to create a lifestyle that accords with her desire. In "Transpoetics in Translation," Liz Rose theorizes the Argentine trans poet Susy Shock's reclamation of the label "Monster." Rose shows how Shock's poem "I, Monster Mine" changes the relation of "monster" from other to self, enabling the othered's agency in the world by claiming it as an "I" that is both queer and desiring, powerful and self-authoring.

If we reexamine "fallen women" – prostitutes, courtesans, the demi-monde (Romantic period slang for those offering sexual promiscuity) – as monstrous, we can begin to see them as free agents rather than victims. Romance novels insist on the victimized status of young women who succumb to sexual activity before marriage, or who succumb to adultery and are disowned by their husbands. These women must go into exile if wealthy enough; if poor they are thrown out of the village, destined for poverty, prostitution, or madness. Perhaps the best-known literary example of the period is Austen's Lydia Bennet in *Pride and Prejudice*, whose elopement with Wickham exposes her to paternal rejection, a damaged reputation, or worse. Austen often includes a minor character, such as Colonel Brandon's ward Eliza in *Sense and Sensibility* (1811), to serve as a warning to other women characters in the novel who are ignoring the rules of decorum to a dangerous degree (here, Marianne Dashwood). Mary Hays plots an entire novel around a heroine who, through sheer class politics, is forced closer and closer to prostitution as the only viable option in *Victim of Prejudice* (1799).

But if we reconceive these women, as well as trans men and cross-dressing individuals who disguised themselves to work as sailors and soldiers, even as thieves, as self-monstering, we get a different picture of people claiming their desire by claiming their otherness as a form of agency they would not otherwise have. Although some women wrote memoirs of their exploits after retiring, much of what we know now comes from archival research. One resource for archival information on women sailors is the Royal Museums at Greenwich; their website makes some of this information available, such as that the largest number of women who disguised themselves as men (presumably quite a number of these were trans men) in order to go to sea or fight in the military did so in the 18th century. Because of the various wars Britain participated in during the century, both the navy and army were hungry for recruits, making it easier for women to apply. Becoming an officer was impossible, so any woman who undertook the adventure did so as a common sailor or army private. They would have seen and participated in fighting first-hand, or if on a trade vessel worked the sails and cargo with the other men, and ate and slept with them while disguising their bodies. Women were known to have fought in the naval battles in the Caribbean (West Indies) and India, both locations important to the backstories of Admiral Croft in Austen's *Persuasion* (1817). There Mrs. Croft explains to another female character about the advantages of living aboard ship with her husband, including the global education received from so much travel.

Women, as we learn from the discussion in *Persuasion*, traveled as officers' wives with their children onboard ship, whether with their husbands or as a form of transport to join with them. The archives show us that women also worked as flag makers, ship painters, ironmongers, nurses, and dockyard rat catchers. Only one of these trades is traditionally female, and yet women were doing the work as women. More sensational, however, were the women who cross-dressed. An interesting case is a young woman forced into the role, Mary Anne Talbot (1778–1808). The 15-year-old heiress and illegitimate daughter of the Earl of Talbot, she suffered the fate of so many heroines of romance novels, abduction by an adventurer. In her case, this was an officer, Captain Bowen, who raped her and then forced her to board a British naval ship en route to Haiti dressed as a cabin boy, "John Talbot." She spent three years as a man on naval ships, working as an officer's cabin boy, powder monkey (loading the cannons with powder before cannonballs were inserted), drummer, "foot boy," and principal cabin boy. She met Admiral Lord Howe aboard the HMS Brunswick, a new warship with 74 cannons, and saw battle in the Caribbean and Flanders (Royal Museums Greenwich website).

Other women were less documented, their male names known but not their birth names or much detail about their lives aboard ship: William Brown, the only Black woman sailor we know enlisted in the British navy, Paul Daniels, Arthur Douglas are among those recorded in naval archives because they were detected as cross-dressed women, but there were undoubtedly many others who escaped detection. Both Byron and Mary Shelley include in their works young female characters who disguise themselves as boys to be near the men they adore. Female desire is the strong factor in these fictional accounts, justifying the cross-dressing which then is revealed (and sometimes punished with the character's early death). This way of translating women's and tran men's adventure lust into sexual desire actually works to de-radicalize a woman's change of gender identity to pursue her own goals. Byron's depiction of the cross-dressing, besotted girl Kaled in his verse Turkish Tale *Lara, A Tale* (1814), who serves as her love interest's page, focuses on her beauty, physical frailty, and tenderness. Her depiction, which translates her heroism into self-sacrifice in the name of love, is a good example of this reductive strategy that effectively counters the memoirs of real-life women sailors and soldiers. It also reduces the risks and dangers involved, since Count Lara is careful to shield his "page," protecting him from the worst of the duels and battling he faces on his journey home from the Near East (now the Middle East). Kaled's gender identity is only revealed when he/she faints at Lara's death from an arrow wound. Mary Shelley indulges in some of this paternalizing strategy in *The Last Man* (1826). There she portrays the beautiful and heroic young Greek woman Evadne as self-destructive when she similarly disguises herself to fight alongside her love interest, the Byronic Lord Raymond. That Shelley's cross-dressed soldier is much more self-destructive than Byron's character and is so while in service to the Byronic Lord Raymond, is an interesting commentary on Shelley's assessment of the renowned poet's attitude towards women's capabilities. As Shelley knew Byron well, her judgment here is both biographical and a critique of patriarchal and paternal ideologies of her day. These are, of course, the very prejudices and ideas that women who went to sea or served in the army were fighting against.

SUMMARY

We see that gender identity is still fluid during the Romantic period. People expressed their identity in ways that could be transitory or confirmed.

- Gender identity was associated with resistance when it expressed an individual's agency.
- The early decades of the Romantic period were ones of freer exploration of desire through "free love," love triangles, and the widespread acceptance of "female friendship."
- Masculinity was also being questioned by writers who worried that fashions (the dandy) and imagination (especially poetry) were effeminizing.
- Children were considered more gender fluid, a flexible attitude toward the child's undeveloped nature that led to the "romantic child" conception.
- The reality of sexual and gender experimentation left victims, who had few options besides suicide or self-exile.
- Only relatively recently have historians recognized the culturally accepted forms of gender nonconformity in the period.
- While feminist writers such as Mary Robinson argued for freer gender expression, non-gender conforming individuals such as Anne Lister found ways to express their identity in socially acceptable ways, even while hiding their private thoughts from friends and family.
- Military and naval records reveal a surprising number of individuals who were revealed to be women after successfully serving as soldiers and sailors. Literary writers reflected this reality through women characters disguised as young men.

FURTHER READING

A history of queer sexual identity that includes the Romantic era is Heyman's *Before We Were Trans*. See Linda Colley on the rise of patriotism: *Britons: Forging of a Nation 1707–1837*. Read more about the Ladies of Llangollen on the Women's History Network. The website dedicated to the letters of Coleridge offers a peek into archival research as well as a deeper dive into the personal lives of several writers of the period. The website "Visit Calderdale" reveals how the secret code that Anne Lister created for her diaries was finally solved:

WEBSITES

The Letters of Samuel Taylor Coleridge. http://stcletters.com/.
Royal Museums Greenwich. https://www.rmg.co.uk/stories/topics/women-who-went-sea-dressed-men.
Visit Calderdale. https://www.visitcalderdale.com/the-secret-diaries-of-anne-lister-cracking-the-crypthand-code/.
Women's History Network. https://womenshistorynetwork.org/the-ladies-of-llangollen/.
Legislation concerning Hampstead Heath: https://www.legislation.gov.uk/ukla/Vict/34-35/77/pdfs/ukla_18710077_en.pdf.

WORKS CITED

Brogan, Stephen. "A 'Monster of Metamorphosis': Reassessing the Chevalier/Chevaliere d'Éon's Change of Gender." In *The Chevalier d'Éon and His Worlds*, edited by Simon Burrows, et al., 81–96. London: Continuum.
Burrows, Simon, et al., eds. *The Chevalier d'Éon and His Worlds: Gender, Espionage and Politics in the Eighteenth Century*. London: Continuum, 2010.
Butler, Judith. *Gender Trouble: Feminism and the Subversion of Identity*. New York: Routledge, 2006.
Coleridge, Samuel Taylor. *Letters of Samuel Taylor Coleridge*. Edited by Ernest Hartley Coleridge. Vol. I. London: Hansebooks, 1895.
Coleridge, Samuel Taylor. *Anima Poetae*. Edited by Ernest Hartley Coleridge. London: Hansebooks, 1898.
Colley, Linda. *Britons: Forging of a Nation 1707–1837*. New Haven: Yale, 1992.
Crompton, Louis. *Byron and Greek Love: Homophobia in 19th-century England*. Swaffham: Gay Men's Press, 1998.
De Quincey, Thomas. *Confessions of an English Opium-Eater*. London: Taylor and Hessey, 1823.
Ewan, Elizabeth, Sue Innes, and Sian Reynolds, eds. *The Biographical Dictionary of Scottish Women*. Edinburgh: Edinburgh University Press, 2007.
Freud, Sigmund. "Some Psychical Consequences of The Anatomical Distinction Between the Sexes." In *The Standard Edition of the Complete Psychological Works of Sigmund Freud*, edited by James Strachey, Vol. 19, 241–58. London: Random House, 2001.
Heyman, Kit. *Before We Were Trans: A New History of Gender*. London: John Murray-Hachette, 2022.

Lister, Anne. *The Secret Diaries of Anne Lister.* Edited by Helena Whitbread. London: Virago Press, 2010.

Robinson, Mary. *A Letter to the Women of England on the Injustice of Mental Subordination*. London: Longmans, 1799.

Rose, Liz. "Transpoetics in Translation: Desire and Feminist Capacity in the Work of Susy Shock." *Transgender Studies Quarterly* 10, no. 1 (2023).

St Clair, William. *The Godwins and the Shelleys: The Biography of a Family.* New York: W. W. Norton, 1989.

Vicinus, Martha. *Intimate Friends: Women Who Loved Women, 1778–1928.* Chicago: University of Chicago, 2004.

Wordsworth, William. "Ode, Intimations of Immortality." In *Poems*, 147–58. London: Longman, Hurst, Rees, and Orme, 1807.

4

THE GOTHIC MODE

INTRODUCTION

Occasionally current events, such as the global pandemic, and subsequent lockdown, safety precautions, and isolation of 2020–2021, produced a very gothic feel to that time of anxiety, with feelings of insecurity about the present and the future, fears for our safety, and for those we love and care about. These heightened emotions, psychologically impactful but externally provoked, can help us understand the **Gothic craze** that flourished at the end of the 18th century in Britain and was such a strong component of British romanticism. It arose while Britain was threatened by revolt in the American colonies and by political unrest in France; enjoying the titillation of literary or artistic terror probably helped people cope with the real terror of revolution abroad and possibly at home.

The gothic was also an important aspect of German romanticism, where gothic stories and plays such as Friedrich Schiller's *The Robbers* (1781) explored the ways that strong passions could influence aesthetic experience. Studying the psychology behind what makes gothics such powerful cultural narratives, no matter when they were written, can help us understand how we are still enthralled by those produced today. Although German gothics were typically critiques of corrupt politics (like *The Robbers*) or patriarchal caste systems (such as August von Kotzebue's *Das Kind der Liebe* (1780), which means "Love Child"), they were received in Britain as works that heightened the emotions in a titillating

DOI: 10.4324/9781032625744-5

way. Wordsworth railed against "sickly German gothics" in the Preface he wrote to the second edition of *The Lyrical Ballads* (1800), the landmark volume of poems he and Coleridge first published in 1798. Gothics, concerned with supernatural doings, are characterized by the loss of boundaries (inside-outside, moral-amoral, human-nonhuman, hallucination-reality) and transgression of principles, mores, prohibitions, social decorum (behavioral rules), and laws.

ARCHITECTURE, POLITICS, MEDIEVALISM, SEXUALITY

The Gothic was more than a subgenre of fiction – our current understanding of "gothic." It was a cultural movement of the late 18th century that, particularly in Britain, was as prevalent in architecture as it was in the arts (plays, poetry, novels, tales, the visual arts, ceramics). Commonly thought to have begun with Horace Walpole's short novel *The Castle of Otranto* (1764), it actually appeared in the architectural Gothic Revival first, and its origins are equally to be found in Eastern Europe, spreading to Germany, and then on to the Continent and Europe; the British gothic spread to the Americas, influencing literary production here, providing African American writers in particular a genre well-suited for modern cultural critique. But we can find traces of it in Dante's *Inferno* and Shakespeare's *Hamlet*, which include incestuous relationships, psychological disorientation, existential doubt, and loss of boundary markers – all key elements for what became the gothic.

Here the gothic will be treated as a Romantic-period phenomenon because this was the first time the Gothic became a major cultural influence (it continues to recur as a cultural form). The gothic also has political implications: when Walpole turned the architectural revitalization of the gothic style's simple, cruder forms into the environment for his fictionalized ghost-inhabited castle Strawberry Hill, he was also transforming the gothic style's association with political radicalism, and its underground association with gay culture, into a ghost story for the general public. *Otranto*'s titillating elements are hard for us to discern, but they led to the rapid popularization of this scandalous formula. The gothic derives its force from several sources: medieval Catholic superstitions concerning devils, witchcraft, and spirit life; folklore and ghost stories; medieval architectural and sculptural forms, as well as remaining Catholic monastery and abbey ruins such as Tintern Abbey; and most importantly, in terms of what makes the gothic continually relevant, its expression of the unconscious as an uninhibited landscape where terrible things can happen. Bram Stoker's *Dracula* is a prime example of this last aspect. As a genre, the gothic is closest to the **quest romance**, the most familiar today being the medieval tales of King Arthur's Knights of the Round Table; the *Raiders of the Lost Ark* (1981) and *Star Wars* (1977–present) films are modern versions of the quest romance. The "dark force," impenetrable evil, and horrific punishments – key features of these films – also threaten quest romance knights *and* gothic heroes and heroines, where darkness signifies demonic forces, and evil can be dark magic or pure human malice. These are also elements of nightmares – unpredictable, incomprehensible, malicious, disorienting visions – that reflect the unconscious attempting to make sense of childhood fears, and the day's occurrences, anxiety, guilt, confusion. The gothic recreates nightmare experiences and exploits the universal fear of brutality, evil, inexplicable events, an uncertain future, and threats to life. But it does so for fun: it's fun to identify with a hero experiencing increasing degrees of paranoia if we can easily put the book down or pause the movie. It's pleasurable to accompany the hero or heroine as they solve the mystery and finish the quest; much of the readerly trepidation relates to inexplicable events or behaviors, and much of the fun lies in anticipating the mystery's explanation.

An important stimulus to the Gothic craze in Britain, therefore, was an increased interest in medieval history and culture caused by a return to Gothic architecture as a signature of British identity. Gothic ruins were the very place to visit and imagine medieval knights, monks, and captive ladies inhabiting the original buildings. And by dusk, it was a fanciful entertainment to not only imagine ghosts of both predators and victims roaming castle or abbey ruins, but even to stage parties there with everyone in medieval dress. Byron delighted in entertaining his university friends at his ancestral home, Newstead Abbey. Dressed as monks, they even ghoulishly drank wine from a monk's skull Byron found on the abbey grounds (Brand 74). Byron was no antiquarian – playacting was his intention. But scholarly antiquarians (men who collected artifacts and manuscripts related to Britain's past) did inspire others to collect medieval armor and weapons, often displaying them on walls in their homes as did Sir Walter Scott. Bishop Thomas Percy collected folk ballads and romances which he published as *Reliques of Ancient English Poetry* in 1775 as part of his endeavor to strengthen a sense of Englishness (Groom 178); works like this also stimulated a resurgence in medieval romances, Arthurian tales, and a sentimentalization of knightly quests and medieval battles that also fed into nationalist nostalgia. Whereas romance and knightly quests were one mode that romantic writers engaged (such as John Keats's 1820 poem *Eve of St. Agnes*), **medievalism** also largely underwrote Gothic novels, plays, even operas. Gothic architecture and gothic literature are inextricably woven together, as in Walpole's foundational *Castle of Otranto.*

Finally, sexuality is a signal reason why gothics were titillating for readers. Illicit sex, mystery, and heightened fear are a potent combination that contributed overpoweringly to the gothic's popularity (Zigarovich 383). For this reason, the craze for political gothics translated from the German gave way to British gothics with recognizable heroes and heroines, and a tantalizing combination of sexual threat and mystery gained hold.

The first gothics were written by writers like Walpole, but also by poets like Coleridge, who wrote several gothic poems including his early masterful "Rime of the Ancient Mariner" (1798). Works like these, which explore the unconscious and dreams, encouraged a flood of works whose writers exploited the increasing taste for sensational literature, something like the general appetite for horror movies today. Some landmark Gothic novels in the sensational vein are Matthew Lewis's *The Monk* (1796), which gave him the moniker "Monk Lewis," and Charles Maturin's *Melmoth the Wanderer* (1820), which employs another gothic trait – the immortal man who is doomed to wander until he can convince another to take his place. The "deal with the devil" motif yoked gothics to hellfire tales stemming back to medieval morality plays and Renaissance revenge tragedies, stories where the protagonist is punished for his sins by being thrown down to hell. Don Juan and

Faust are characters in this lineage. Maturin's work inspired Oscar Wilde, who was Maturin's great nephew, to write his own gothic about the immortal man and a deal with the devil, *The Picture of Dorian Gray* (1891).

Because such works were usually written by men and included bloodshed, incest, adultery, and supernatural elements, they were termed by women writers "**horror gothics**." The feminine version was termed "**terror gothics**," with the idea that terror is an emotion aroused by the unknown, but with sufficient logic and detective work the heroine can find a rational explanation for the mysteries she encounters (Hoeveler 15). We can see the male gothic, then, as centered on unconscious desires and the supernatural, and the female gothic as centered on reason. Male gothics explore illicit desire, heightened rage, and other psychological states that lay outside the bounds of decorum. Female gothics for the most part center on what lies hidden behind decorum: spousal abuse, patriarchal power, dictatorial parents, disinherited children, and heiress hunters. Whereas the male gothic always takes place in a corrupt society, the female gothic, as exemplified in Ann Radcliffe's novels, purposely locates much of the novel in nature and elevates the form by using the romantic themes of natural beauty, the sublime in nature, the poetic imagination, individual agency, and personal liberties.

GHOSTS, VAMPIRES, DECADENCE, AND HEROISM

Gothic novels and poetry exploit the fear of restless spirits inhabiting old ruins. A favorite conceit was of ghosts of the nuns and monks who had lived in the monasteries torn down on the order of Henry VIII when he broke with the Catholic Church and claimed the lands that had belonged to it. To visit ruins in the night was to invite apparitional encounters. In *Castle of Otranto*, Walpole used a ghost who could intervene in human life to avenge himself and restore legitimacy to his family. In her best-known novel, *Mysteries of Udolpho* (1794), Radcliffe made ghosts, or the rumor of them, central to her gothic tale of spousal abuse and heiress abduction. Because gothics needed landscapes where ghosts, abuses of various kinds, medieval settings or connotations, and other set piece elements, they were usually set in Catholic countries such as Italy or Spain and often set in the medieval past.

One version of the male horror gothic was the vampire story. Vampires give the myth of immortal man, as in Maturin's *Melmoth the Wanderer*, a dark twist. The curse that the wanderer needs to pass onto another man to free himself from a devil's bargain is transformed into the vampire's bite, and an undead version of immortality. In both cases, the curse requires the undying or undead to survive at the expense of the living. In this sense, the vampire is related to the vengeful ghost, but instead of restoring the honor of an aristocratic or royal family as in *Castle of Otranto*, the vampire – usually of aristocratic birth – destroys a family, usually upper middling class. The vampire tale, then, is closer to the female terror gothic, which also revolves around aristocratic corruption and its attacks on bourgeois wealth and family values through heiress abduction (a theme also of domestic romances dating back to Samuel Richardson's 1748 landmark novel *Clarissa*). Such novels reflected the very real fears of the middling classes that the wealth they produced through commerce and manufacture was unstable in relation to the landed wealth of the aristocracy, since banks were not secured by the government and a bank's failure meant losing one's own savings. Aristocratic families that had become impoverished due to bad management of the lands, or the gambling and spending habits of their heirs, were a menace to the middle-class imagination. Novels were where these fears could be played out. The few documented cases of actual heiress abductions, together with the very real need to marry into middle-class fortunes of aristocratic younger sons who didn't inherit their father's estates, were a potent source of anxiety. Radcliffe's novels always end with the heroine discovering she is heiress to a family fortune and estate, secure in both her financial future and in the love of the hero who has attempted her rescue. That she must defeat the aristocratic villain herself is a fine riposte to domestic romances like *Clarissa* where the heroine's only recourse by the end is to die, having been dishonored by her abductor. But the reality was that the decadence of aristocrats was legion in the period.

Both men and women gambled at parties; men gambled in their clubs. Fortunes were won and lost in the same night. Georgiana, Duchess of Devonshire, was the beautiful young wife of the Duke, the largest landholder in England in the Romantic period and far wealthier than the king. She became addicted to gambling and had to be rescued by her husband numerous times for excessive debts (Foreman 234–5, 245–8). Wealthy women could hold all-female gambling parties. Likewise, because it was organized by arranged marriages between important families to combine power and land, aristocratic life was rife with affairs and adulterous assignations. **Pleasure gardens** like Vauxhall and Ranelagh, both near the Thames River, had large gardens where couples could disappear for a brief time, and masquerade balls were particularly useful for assignations since identities were literally masked. The costumes enhanced sexual allure so that spur-of-the-moment assignations were also possible.

Unsurprisingly, then, the first vampire tale begins at just such entertainments: John Polidori's "The Vampyre" (1819). (John Stagg's *The Vampyre* appeared in 1810, but Polidori's was the vampire version that caught on.) Famously, the story originated in the same storytelling contest that produced *Frankenstein*. Polidori was Byron's attending physician on his travels, and Byron was staying by Lake Geneva, where he became intimate with Percy Shelley, Mary Godwin (later Shelley), and Mary's half-sister Claire Clairmont, with whom Byron had an affair. During the stormy, wet summer the group met frequently, and one night during a severe thunderstorm they entertained themselves by reading aloud German ghost stories. The contest's rules were that each participant was to produce something as an outcome of the evening's entertainment, but the only completed works were "The Vampyre" and *Frankenstein*.

In Polidori's tale, Lord Ruthven is a British nobleman whose haughty bearing and general disdain for society show him to be based on Byron himself. Because the resemblance is so close, Ruthven's vampirism was rumored to be Byron's own, creating an uncomfortable blurring of gossip – about Byron's unorthodox sexual proclivities, his extravagant lifestyle, and his marriage to a wealthy middle-class heiress to shore up his own depleted fortune

– and fantasy fiction. Like Byron, the handsome Lord Ruthven is the very model of the suave, charismatic aristocrat who does not, like Stoker's Dracula, show his age or indicate in any way that he is not a man of the times. Polidori's tale begins with acknowledging that the vampire legend originated in the Middle East (Byron had written about his travels to Turkish-influenced Albania and had included an anecdote of vampires in his 1813 Turkish Tale "The Giaour"). Ruthven enters London high society as a nobleman more "remarkable for his singularities, than his rank."

> He gazed upon the mirth around him, as if he could not participate therein ... Those who felt this sensation of awe, could not explain whence it arose: some attributed it to the dead grey eye, which, fixing upon the object's face, did not seem to penetrate, and at one glance to pierce through to the inward workings of the heart; but fell upon the cheek with a leaden ray that weighed upon the skin it could not pass.
> (para. 1)

This characteristic description of the vampire – neither of this world nor out of it, disdainful of other people but penetrating their secrets with his gaze – becomes the template for the modern vampire character, as opposed to inhuman, monstrous depictions of vampires as in "The Giaour" and other references to Arabic versions of the creature.

Ruthven befriends a newcomer, Aubrey, who together with his sister has been left orphaned by their wealthy middle-class parents. Aubrey has come to complete his education by experiencing London society, and so also agrees to travel with Ruthven as his companion. Unfortunately, growing up under guardians' careless oversight, Aubrey had "cultivated more his imagination than his judgment. He had, hence, that high romantic feeling of honour and candour, which daily ruins so many milliners' apprentices" (para. 2). Aubrey's innocence and idealism contrast sharply with Ruthven's world-weariness; his education into the decadence of society via Ruthven becomes an analogue for his growing awareness that Ruthven is not what he seems. Although they separate in Rome after Aubrey is disgusted by Ruthven's decadence, they meet up again in Greece where, eerily, Ruthven finds him after Aubrey has fallen in love with the beautiful Ianthe. It is Ianthe who tells him of the vampire legend, cautioning him not to travel through the forest after sundown. He ignores her, and on his return finds her bloodied body there, bite marks on her neck. After a nervous illness resulting from finding the body, Aubrey is reunited with Ruthven. The pair recommence their travels but are attacked by robbers, and Ruthven is fatally wounded. He demands Aubrey not mention his death for a year (a common trope of tales of immortal men). On Aubrey's return to London, a healthy Ruthven is already there, wooing Miss Aubrey, his sister. Their wedding is set for the day before Aubrey's oath expires, and so his necessarily vague warnings aren't taken seriously, his guardians assuming him temporarily deranged. The story ends with Aubrey unsure of his own sanity, and the line between the story as reality or Aubrey's fevered imagination blurred.

An interesting contrast to Polidori's vampire tale is Coleridge's much earlier enigmatic poem "Christabel" (1800). Here, Coleridge mixes medieval romance with witchcraft and a sexuality that suggests vampirism, although of the spirit rather than blood, and, therefore, more allied with hypnotic spells. The poem recounts Christabel's encounter with the Lady Geraldine, who arrives alone, seemingly the abducted victim of rogues. Christabel invites the lady in and shares her bed with her for the night. By day, Geraldine claims to be the daughter of a friend of Sir Leoline, Christabel's father, but by night she seems to be a different creature altogether. Christabel discovered the distressed lady when she went to pray for her lover's safety at the huge oak tree. With her own mother dead, Christabel sees in Geraldine a comforting substitute. But immediately there are portents of evil: Geraldine cannot cross the castle's threshold, the same boundary between inside and outside that vampires and other supernatural creatures cannot cross without invitation.

> The lady sank, belike through pain,
> And Christabel with might and main
> Lifted her up, a weary weight,
> Over the threshold of the gate.
>
> *(129–32)*

When the two pass the great hall's fireplace, dying embers flame up again at Geraldine's presence, and when they arrive at her bedchamber and Christabel lights the lamp, suddenly "Geraldine, in wretched plight, / Sank down upon the floor below" (188–9). Then, Geraldine sees an apparition and appears to wildly call out to Christabel's dead mother. Christabel interprets this as delirium, rather than her mother's ghost attempting to protect her, and prepares for bed with the stranger, but she is shocked when Geraldine disrobes: "Behold! her bosom and half her side— / A sight to dream of, not to tell! / O shield her! shield sweet Christabel!" (152–4). We never learn why the sight is so disturbing (Is Geraldine much older than she seems? Is she part demonic? Or is her body bewitchingly beautiful?) but from then on Christabel is deeply disturbed and suspicious of who Geraldine is or what she wants.

The unfinished poem is hauntingly unfinished, with Christabel frustrated in attempting to warn her father the next day of Geraldine's uncanniness. A widower, Sir Leoline clearly takes a fancy to Geraldine, and the threat of this mysterious creature becoming her stepmother makes the provisional ending a potent combination of fairy tale's wicked stepmother, medieval tales of witchcraft, the hint of lesbian sex ("A sight to dream of, not to tell!" 153), and a touch of vampirism. The combination is monstrous in the gothic sense of all prohibitions crossed. The male gothic vividly depicts incestuous desire, queer sexual activity, polyamory, as well as murderous rage, psychotic hallucinations, sibling rivalry, patricide and fratricide, and physical and psychological abuse, even torture. The female gothic hints that, since all of these have happened in the past, and can be allied with patriarchal and hierarchical power struggles, it is possible they are also part of the prehistory of the current story, but that despite suggestions that such transgressions may still be going on, any villainy is of the human and not nonhuman type.

William Beckford's *Vathek* (1786), which explores monstrousness, lack of inhibitions, and transgressive behaviors, is one of the best Gothics for seeing how witchery, illicit sex, and transgression work to captivate readers' attention. Beckford's signature work is both an "Oriental" tale and a gothic. Using the themes and settings of Orientalist tales (Middle Eastern settings and characters similar to those in the influential translations of the *Thousand and One Nights*), *Vathek* exploits the different sexual mores of Middle

Eastern cultures – particularly harems and eunuchs – along with the absolute power of sultans and emperors and the historical association of ancient Mediterranean cultures with astrology, astronomy, alchemy, and magic. All these elements play important roles in the novel, with the most malignant versions of them associated with Vathek's imperious mother, the power behind her effeminate son's throne. Like "Christabel," this work highlights female evil and offers a strong contrast to male horror gothics, which are associated, like vampire tales, with male evil. Like "Christabel," *Vathek* poses female power against male weakness; Vathek is so self-indulgent he treats himself like a child, and Sir Leoline is too susceptible to female charm, even when this is manipulative and insincere.

Although Gothics are typified by a patriarchal villain, *Vathek* features a mother who functions as this patriarch. The caliph Vathek relies on his mother Carathis, adept in astrology and dark magic, to advise him. He does so especially when his people rebel at his increasingly strange demands. The instigator of these demands, a genii-like stranger and the mysterious messages on his magical sword, belongs to the Arabian tale genre, but Vathek's insatiable greed and his mother's desire for power over both natural and supernatural realms lead to acts of pure evil, reenacting the worst of human history such as the betrayal of innocent people, human sacrifice by fire, infanticide, transgressive love, and female abduction. As an "Oriental" tale, harems and eunuchs play a large role in the story, but as a gothic it is what Carathis does in her tower that haunts the imagination. A practitioner of Zoroastrianism, an ancient Persian religion that worships fire, Carathis commits atrocities to gain the spirits' aid in her plans. As with most male gothics, Vathek and his beloved arrive in Hell (the Palace of Eblis), but it is Carathis who, in her ceaseless demand for more power, attempts to rob Eblis's magic treasures, only to die by hellfire: "Instantaneously, the haughty forehead of the intrepid princess became corrugated with agony; she uttered a tremendous yell, and fixed—no more to be withdrawn—her right hand upon her heart, which was become a receptacle of eternal fire" (Beckford, 147). Vathek's passive personality contrasts strongly with his mother's self-agency, yet she is not the novel's main character. She is the manifestation of human evil, the Geraldine-like witch who seeks to dominate others, manipulating them to do her bidding. Male gothics generally focus on evil male characters and passive female ones, but *Vathek* and "Christabel" stand out as exemplars of cultural fears of female desire and power.

A Gothic that uses some of the same motifs as *Vathek* is Byron's *Manfred* (c. 1816–1817). A closet drama in verse, *Manfred* is not about female power but about male desire that is both incestuous and power-hungry (Vathek and Carathis in one). Manfred, an aristocrat and the last remaining member of his family, is a medieval astronomer and **alchemist** who, like Carathis, engages in Zoroastrian rituals and secret knowledge to force the elements and spirits to obey him. But he has a guilty secret that he must come to terms with; although never revealed, he hints at his love for his sister, and that he caused her self-inflicted death. Though he has worked hard for the alchemist's goal of eternal life, now Manfred wants death to quell his guilt-ridden memories. Defying the intervention of the pious Abbot of St. Maurice, Manfred faces his end when he is summoned by Arimanes, the Zoroastrian destructive spirit. The clear division between male evil, manifested in Manfred's self-centered quest for power, and female victimization that Byron employs, pares down the patriarchal gendering that underlies the Gothic, revealing it clearly, whereas Beckford's *Vathek* and Coleridge's "Christabel" complicate these gender stereotypes. But both male horror gothics and female terror gothics employ evil female characters to show malevolence as a fully human trait that can appear in anyone; the person you encounter on the street is not what they appear, these stories warn. Beware the mother as well as the father; either can be the evil powermonger or perverse relation.

Radcliffe's novels are prime examples of the female terror gothic, and while also including evil female characters, she pointedly employs active female protagonists who must defeat patriarchal villains. Those villains, aristocratic and debt-ridden, pursue or capture the heroine not for sexual purposes (although she is made vulnerable to sexual threat by such pursuit and capture), but for her fortune. Sometimes Radcliffe makes a novel's mystery the orphaned heroine's identity as a wealthy heiress with an estate, that information having been hidden from her by those scheming to take her wealth for themselves. This theme of the abducted heiress, along with decadent impoverished aristocrats (or pretenders who have usurped the position), aligns Radcliffe's female gothics with the domestic romance because of its upper middle-class anxieties about social status, rank, and power. Although the heroines are usually revealed to be aristocrats' daughters, they are presumed middling class through most of the novel, and the narrative's anxieties over stolen inheritance are how middle-class readers identify with the heroine. Male gothics, by contrast, usually feature protagonists from aristocratic families who either pursue the dream of achieving unnatural power (as Manfred does) or who become the victim of institutional corruption, usually the medieval Catholic Church.

Although *Mysteries of Udolpho* is probably Radcliffe's best-known novel, her first successful gothic, *Romance of the Forest* (1791), is the most contemporaneous in that it opens with a group of people fleeing Paris, echoing the desperate escapes from that city during the early years of the French Revolution. The La Mottes and their two servants are only escaping creditors, however. Waylaid by criminals in the dark, Mme. La Motte and the servants stay in the carriage while Pierre La Motte leaves and, following a light, finds a small house where he asks to stay the night. Once in his bedroom, however, his strange host locks his door and later drags a beautiful young girl into the room, telling Pierre he must take her with him because he never wants to see her again. Pierre consents, and he and Adeline – the novel's heroine – are conveyed back to the carriage. The novel begins, then, with the heroine thrust on others after being held captive, an inversion of standard abduction tales that captures the reader's interest as they try to unravel the mystery of Adeline's presence in the criminal's house and her violent ejection from it. With Adeline, the La Mottes then happen on an abandoned abbey in the forest and begin to live there secretly. There, they discover a skeleton in a chest hidden in the labyrinth-like basement, a plot development that is complicated by the love attentions of two young lovers and a Marquis for Adeline and the sexual jealousies of the La Mottes. Adeline also finds an ancient manuscript in the abbey, written by a man expecting his imminent death, and whose skeleton is possibly his remains. After various intrigues the Marquis reveals that he wants to kill Adeline, not marry her. Because this is a theme that occurs in male gothics, it shows how Radcliffe uses elements of male gothics to make a point about the very real disparities in affective relationships between aristocratic and middling classes. Like the vampire, who marries to consume his bride–victim, the Marquis woos to conceal the fact that he is no aristocrat but rather the murderer of her father, and having stolen his fortune, intends to have Adeline murdered in order to conceal his illegal claim on her inheritance. That he is thwarted in his designs transforms his evil into a very human type, terrible but not demonic.

THE GOTHIC AS CULTURAL UNCONSCIOUS

This section focuses on the male horror gothic, including one written by a woman; unlike Radcliffe's terror gothics, the demonic nature of the horror gothic reveals something about the cultural fears of the period. The horror gothic begins with Walpole's *Castle of Otranto*, a short novel that sets out two important tropes for the genre. First, the castle itself manifests the gothic space of medieval architecture, with its dungeons below ground and maze-like basement passages that connect with tunnels to other buildings, where characters can become lost, disoriented, or held captive. Second, the hallucinatory atmosphere of the gothic, in which supernatural events are important plot elements. *Otranto* also features a patriarch who, like Radcliffe's Marquis, had murdered Alfonso, the rightful patriarch and assumed his position. His son, Manfred, is the current lord and has arranged a marriage for his heir, Conrad, to the Princess Isabella to gain her lands. The novel begins with a gigantic knight's helmet thrown down on the courtyard where it kills Conrad just after the marriage ceremony. Other occult elements include a giant armored leg that the servants see in an upstairs room and a gigantic sword that Isabella's father discovers buried in a forest, both it is finally revealed to belong to Alfonso's ghost. The sword is engraved with a prophecy concerning Isabella's safety and the restoration of Otranto to its rightful heir. It is revealed that the young lover of Isabella, Theodore, who has a mysterious past, is that heir, Alfonso's grandson. This plot, concerning rightful inheritance and true love versus arranged marriage, is complicated by Manfred's manipulations to secure Isabella's fortune. First, he imprisons his wife Hippolita and then forces Father Jerome to divorce them so that he can marry Isabella himself. This is incestuous, since she is now his daughter-in-law, another major trope of the male gothic. It is also the model for gothics like *Romance of the Forest,* where the Marquis is a pretender, murdering the rightful Marquis and assuming his position. Finally, it is revealed that not only is Theodore Alfonso's grandson, but Isabella's father is his closest surviving male relative. This explains why Alfonso's ghost protects Isabella by killing the innocent Conrad at their wedding ceremony, and why he intervenes in leading her father to the sword.

Another influential male horror gothic, *The Monk* (1796), became so popular that its author, Matthew Lewis, became known as "Monk Lewis." But initially, the novel shocked its readers; despite the example of *Castle of Otranto*, the public was not yet ready for a plot revolving around an initially pious monk's ravenous appetite for sex. Sexually explicit, the novel tells the story of Ambrosio, a celebrated monk who first is reluctantly drawn into a secret affair with a young admirer, Matilda, who has disguised herself as a monk to be close to him. Tiring of her and her devotion, he then hopes to seduce Antonia; Matilda aids him through witchcraft, which she has already used to seduce Ambrosio. In the cemetery, she calls forth Lucifer, who gives her a magic herb that allows Ambrosio to open any door and to rape Antonia without her knowledge. On the verge of the rape, her mother enters the room and Ambrosio kills her. Later, tired of Antonia, Ambrosio murders her as well. Interrogated by the Spanish Inquisitors, Matilda first confesses her guilt and is sentenced to being burnt at the stake, and then Ambrosio, who first resists but then, faced with torture, confesses. Both decide to sell their souls to Lucifer in return for freedom from their prison cells, but Matilda is canny enough to also ask for life, whereas Ambrosio only asks for freedom. Lucifer maniacally carries him to the sky and drops him on the rocks, a more horribly painful death than fire since it takes him six days to die – his soul condemned to hell for eternity.

This shocking tale of errant sexual desire, incest, and matricide (Lucifer informs Ambrosio that Antonia's mother was also his mother, revealing that he murdered his mother and sister), witchcraft, sacrilege, murder, and unwed sex among several other clerical characters, sets the tone for male horror gothics. They revel in uninhibited desires, the very stuff of the unconscious that dreams and uncontrollable urges reveal. And they involve the corruption of institutions like the Catholic Church and aristocratic hierarchy. What would happen, then, if a woman writer decided to write one? This was what Charlotte Dacre decided to do.

Just a few years after Monk Lewis's shocking debut novel appeared, Dacre published her horror gothic *Zofloya; or The Moor* (1806). Criticized in the reviews for being derivative of *The Monk*, Dacre's novel is nevertheless a fascinating example of women's assertion of female desire during a period when it was scandalous to even suggest such a thing (Airey 224; Moreno 420; Davison 32). *Zofloya* is set in 16th-century Venice, when the Venetian Republic was a powerful Mediterranean force. Dacre's heroine is Victoria de Loredani, the very beautiful but indulged daughter of the Marchese di Loredani and his wife, Laurina. Used to getting her way, Victoria spurns the local youths; her mother is then seduced by the Marchese's friend Count Ardolph and elopes with him. A year later Ardolph returns to Venice, chances on the Marchese in the dark and is challenged to a duel of honor. Not intending to, Ardolph kills his friend, and Victoria comes under his and her mother's guardianship. Joining them, Victoria decides that she wants to control her own destiny and sets her eye on Count Berenza. First becoming his mistress, she then manipulates him into marrying her. So far, this is nothing like *The Monk*. But, once Victoria tastes her own power, everything changes: she eventually murders her husband by slow poison because she lusts for his young brother Henriquez, who is engaged to Lilla. Both the poison and subsequent magical potions and devices are supplied by Zofloya, the handsome Moorish servant of Henriquez. Previous to this, Zofloya had apparently drowned, but his reappearance goes unquestioned; in the final section of the novel, it is revealed that this Zofloya replaced the original and is the devil. His magic potions include one that allows Victoria to assume the appearance of Lilla so she can seduce Henriquez without his awareness. That he is willing to have sex with "Lilla" before marriage is elided in the narrative; it is Victoria's sexual desire that is central to the plot. More deeds of cruelty and desire follow, revealing Victoria's true nature. A more believable version of *The Monk*'s Matilda, who always acts to promote Ambrosio's desire, Victoria portrays female desire as female-centered and a full expression of female agency.

DELICIOUS TERROR

Jane Austen's *Northanger Abbey* (1818; composed 1803) depicts the delicious terror of reading a gothic, Radcliffe's *Mysteries of Udolpho* (1794). Catherine Morland can hardly contain her impatience from one reading session to another, her pleasure doubled by discussing plot revelations with Isabella, and tripled through anticipation. The fear she hopes to experience at Northanger Abbey will be a heightened version of the narrative tension and suspense she experiences reading the novel. James Gillray caricatures this delicious fear in "Tales of Wonder!" (1801), the title of Matthew Lewis's 1801 collection of gothic tales (see link in Works Cited). Austen uses that titillation to parody female gothics, particularly Radcliffe's *Udolpho.* In it, Emily St. Aubert is forced to go with her guardians to the castle Udolpho; frightened by unusual noises and eerie music, she faces the castle's biggest mystery, a black veil that hides a dark secret. When Emily lifts the veil, she sees something so horrifying and incomprehensible that she faints. Catherine, whose excitement at this scene is uncontainable, hopes to find a similar mystery to solve at Northanger. But Austen shows how the everyday can be more dangerous than imagined threats: her brother's friend John Thorpe, in attempting to woo the uninterested Catherine, effectively abducts her for a pleasure ride in his curricle – a carriage so small that occupying it with an unrelated man was both improper and dangerous to her reputation. And in the novel's climax, Northanger's patriarch sends her away in a stagecoach without a chaperone or guide, and without money. This puts the deserted Catherine in real danger on the long journey home: alone in a public coach, and stopping at inns to change coach routes, exposed her to thieves, sexual attack, and simply losing her way without funds to purchase a new ticket. Any terrible happenings she hoped to uncover at the abbey (what she finds is patriarchal contempt for a wife's or children's emotional needs – another gothic theme) were more commonplace in real life at the time than abduction or desertion.

But Austen captures so effectively Catherine's investment in the gothic imagination that we feel her excitement in readerly terror in this exchange with Isabella:

> "I have been reading it [Udolpho] ever since I woke; and I am got to the black veil."
> "Are you, indeed? How delightful! Oh! I would not tell you what is behind the black veil for the world! Are not you wild to know?"
> "Oh! Yes, quite; what can it be? But do not tell me—I would not be told upon any
> account. I know it must be a skeleton, I am sure it is Laurentina's skeleton. Oh! I am delighted with the book! I should like to spend my whole life in reading it. I assure you, if it had not been to meet you, I would not have come away from it for all the world."
>
> *(61)*

Although Austen lampoons her heroine's enthusiasm, readers loved gothic suspense and terror as much as we do today. Vampire stories enhanced this terror by making the supernatural element seem entirely plausible; the dead come back to life embodied rather than as ghosts, feeding on the living rather than merely attempting communication. Stories of premature burial of comatose persons were alarming enough. What if a truly dead person returned, interacting with the living in nearly normal ways, even wedding a victim before drinking her blood?

This is the gist of Polidori's "The Vampyre": Stoker heightens that allure in his Victorian vampire novel. The sex appeal of Lord Ruthven, so magnetizing for women but also aimed homosexually at young men like Aubrey, reveals an aspect of the vampire tale that, like Gothic architecture, might go unnoticed. The vampire has close resemblance to the conservative myth of the homosexual or lesbian who lures and then grooms innocent young victims. We might view the vampire tale as a culturally coded cautionary tale of such a threat to middling-class mores that, even more than the gothic generally, uses sexual threat to not just titillate but also warn the reader. Clearly, the exhilarating thrill of sexual scariness won out over such cautions. That allure and compelling quality combined with horror at his otherness are quintessential traits of the gothic villain. Milton's epic poem *Paradise Lost* begins with the archangel Lucifer battling God for dominion; losing, he and his comrade angels fall to earth where he transforms into the horrific Satan. The gothic revives the idea that Satan still retains some angelic beauty, which gothic villains inherit in the form of charismatic or seductive personalities. Not all Romantic period gothics utilize these features for their villains, but they all rely on this association between the compelling anti-hero, whether villain or vampire, and his charismatic gaze. One way to understand the cultural implications of the compelling gaze as associated with lordly behavior and aristocratic decadence *and* sexual allure is to look at other ways in which being compelled by invisible means was also playing out in social activities.

"**Mesmerism**" was highly popular in the Romantic period, connected to hypnotism (the vampire's gaze) and the theory of "soul sleep" (the soul becomes dormant after death but not dissolved). Mesmerism arose from scientific experimentation with electromagnetism. It was also known as "animal magnetism," and was invented by the German doctor Franz Mesmer in the 1700s; "**vitalism**" was the 19th-century theory that developed from it. A popular theory was that the attraction–rejection effect of magnets was believed to extend to electromagnetic fields between bodies, whether these were human or included natural bodies such as trees. "Doctors" encouraged mystical belief that coordinating these effects between bodies could be curative, and it became a popular craze to engage in group therapy this way. Hypnotism, by contrast, occurred within the body–mind of the subject; the nervous system is calmed and regulated by the hypnotist through some manipulation of the subject's consciousness. Whereas mesmerism was denounced by the mid-1800s as being too associated with the occult, as was the developing fad for séances (in which the medium also controls mind-body experiences), hypnotism was considered scientifically based and medically effective.

And yet writers were quick to see the gothic implications of all these practices since the medium or doctor was in a powerful position of control. Even mesmerism, although eventually debunked as mysticism rather than science, survives today as the character trait "animal magnetism." We sense a man has this physical attraction if his gaze compels others to feel sexy and he begins to seem sexy himself, even if not handsome. In a gothic, a charismatic man with this trait is one whose gaze is both sexy and demonic. The literary tradition of malicious characters having an "evil eye" or controlling stare, or a dead gaze (as Lord Ruthven does in Polidori's "Vampyre"), has precedence in Middle Eastern tales, but also Renaissance depictions of alchemists – proto-scientists who combined basic chemistry with occult rituals to find the elixir of immortal life as a universal panacea or cure, and for a method for turning base metals into gold. These twin desires – for immortality and endless wealth – were really desires for power, as William Godwin, like other writers of gothics with alchemy as a plot device, realized in his novel *St. Leon; A Tale of the Seventeenth Century* (1799). *St. Leon* influenced Godwin's daughter Mary's first novel *Frankenstein*. There, Victor studies alchemy in his father's library, not realizing it had been debunked by modern science. Yet alchemical theories were what allowed Victor to elevate current scientific knowledge to new heights to create immortal life by creating a human through assemblage rather than natural birth. Alchemy was therefore closely associated with bargains with the devil as represented in Maturin's *Melmoth* and Wilde's *Portrait of Dorian Gray*, where immortality and knowledge rather than gold were the gifts that ultimately backfired on those wanting a piece of divine power.

It was the uncanny character, someone with a powerful or lordly presence, more than alchemists, who were the true model for literary figures such as Lord Ruthven and Dracula. The gothic villain, aristocrat and patriarch, and in male horror gothics involved in unholy doings and intimate with the devil, also has the powerful stare that compels obedience from others. Historically, alchemists like Paracelsus and Albertus Magnus (both of whom Victor Frankenstein studied) were scholars, usually from the middling classes. Byron's protagonist in his closet drama *Manfred* is an exception; Manfred is an aristocrat whose motivation for his alchemy competes with his guilt over incestuous love and his sister's death. He is both gothic villain and gothic hero combined. But because his sister's death is never explained, and because Manfred alludes to her so hesitantly, there is a sense that he has drained her of life. As such, Manfred helps us understand how vampires can be both alluring and heroic, whereas truly gothic villains such as Walpole's in *Castle of Otranto* (also named Manfred) are never the hero but always the antagonist to be defeated.

SUMMARY

The Gothic mode has enduring appeal; we love to be scared by scenarios drawn from the human unconscious. The following points convey the gothic's pertinence and appeal.

- The Gothic craze occurred during the early years of the Romantic period just when the threat of revolution created political instability.
- German Gothic had a different cause, arising from a psychologized return to the medieval past.
- The British Gothic mode first appeared architecturally, although even here there were political undertones.
- All Gothic productions include medieval topoi, political implications (a return to harsh patriarchy, oppression, tyranny), nightmare scenarios, unconscious desires, and sexuality.
- British Gothics can be divided into horror gothics (with hellfire and incestuous desire) and terror gothics (where the heroine uncovers a dastardly plot to steal her inheritance, but where the aesthetic of the sublime and beautiful counter gothic elements).
- Gothics are usually placed in Catholic countries such as France or Italy in order to distance the nightmarish events of the plots, but ruins in the Gothic style as well as Gothic Revival buildings could be found throughout Britain and helped inaugurate the gothic imagination.
- Gothics include the vampire story, and gothic elements can be found in numerous other genres.

FURTHER READING

See Punter's *The Literature of Terror* for an overview of the genre, as well as Spooner and McEvoy's *Routledge Companion to Gothic.* Other very readable overviews are Punter and Byron's *The Gothic* and Duggett's *Gothic Romanticism.* See also Hoeveler's *Gothic Feminism.* Jillian Dinkle's gothic interior design gives a sense of why Romantic-period homeowners wanted Gothic elements inside or outside their houses. Fay's *Romantic Medievalism* explores the various versions of the medieval available during the period. The Wikipedia entry on the gothic provides sections on other national literatures, such as Russian gothic, and important genres such as Southern gothic (ie, William Faulkner, Eudora Welty), and contemporary gothic literature and film.

WEBSITES

New York Public Library: A Brief History of Gothic Horror. https://www.nypl.org/blog/2018/10/18/brief-history-gothic-horror.

Wikipedia: Gothic Fiction. https://en.wikipedia.org/wiki/Gothic_fiction.

V&A: The Gothic Style—An Introduction. https://www.vam.ac.uk/articles/the-gothic-style-an-introduction?srsltid=AfmBOop23-PHxLJewXvubrjkeBNVxVCTlXdNO9OQKbmx03Egy0goqoA2.

WORKS CITED

Airey, Jennifer. "'He Bears No Rival Near the Throne': Male Narcissism and Early Feminism in the Works of Charlotte Dacre." *Eighteenth-Century Fiction* 30, no. 2 (Winter 2017–18): 223–41.

Austen, Jane. *Northanger Abbey.* Edited by Claire Grogan, 2nd ed. Peterborough: Broadview, 2002.

Beckford, William. *Vathek.* Edited by Kenneth Graham. Peterborough: Broadview, 2001.

Brand, Emily. *The Fall of the House of Byron.* London: John Murray, 2020.

Coleridge, Samuel Taylor. *Christabel, A Facsimile of the Manuscript.* Edited by Ernest Hartley Coleridge. London: Henry Frowde, 1907.

Davison, Carol Margaret. "Getting Their Knickers in a Twist: Contesting the 'Female Gothic' in Charlotte Dacre's *Zofloya*." *Gothic Studies* 11, no. 1 (2009): 32–45.

Dinkle, Jillian. "Jillian Dinkel Reimagines a Traditional English Home Through a Modern Gothic Lens." *Aspire Design and Home*, 2026. https://

aspiremetro.com/jillian-dinkel-reimagines-a-traditional-english-home-through-a-modern-gothic-lens/.

Duggett, Tom. *Gothic Romanticism Wordsworth, Architecture, Politics, Form*. Basingstoke: Palgrave Macmillan, 2010.

Fay, Elizabeth. *Romantic Medievalism: History and the Romantic Literary Ideal*. Basingstoke: Palgrave Macmillan, 2002.

Foreman, Amanda. *Georgiana: Duchess of Devonshire*. New York: Random House, 1998.

Gillray, James. "Tales of Wonder!" (1801). https://www.metmuseum.org/art/collection/search/853073.

Groom, Nick. *The Making of Percy's Reliques*. Oxford: Clarendon Press, 1999.

Hoeveler, Diane. *Gothic Feminism: The Professionalization of Gender from Charlotte Smith to the Brontës*. Philadelphia: Pennsylvania State University Press, 1998.

Lewis, Matthew Gregory. *Tales of Wonder*. Edited by Douglass H. Thomson. Peterborough: Broadview, 2010.

Moreno, Beatriz González. "Gothic Excess and Aesthetic Ambiguity in Charlotte Dacre's *Zofloya*." *Women's Writing* 14, no. 3 (2007): 419–34.

Polidori, John. *The Vampyre*. London: Henry Colburn Publications, 1819. https://gutenberg.org/files/6087/6087-h/6087-h.htm.

Punter, David. *The Literature of Terror: A History of Gothic Fictions from 1765 to the Present Day*. London: Longman, 1996.

Punter, David and Glennis Byron. *The Gothic*. Oxford: Blackwell, 2004.

Spooner, Catherine, and Emma McEvoy, eds. *The Routledge Companion to Gothic*. London: Routledge, 2007.

Zigarovich, Jolene. "Gothic and the History of Sexuality." In *The Cambridge History of the Gothic*, edited by Angela Wright and Dale Townshend, 382–405. Cambridge: Cambridge University Press, 2020.

5

HISTORY, SCIENCE, AND THE FUTURE

INTRODUCTION

To 21st-century readers it might not seem that history and the future are necessarily connected, or that science has anything to do with either. Yet in the Romantic era, and indeed stretching back even to the Renaissance, these topics were neither discrete nor considered separately from each other. In the Renaissance, medieval alchemy (which sought to change the present and future through alchemical science) began to give way to natural philosophy and astronomy. "**Natural philosophy**" and "**natural history**" were the branches of learning that pursued scientific research, which was as much speculative and therefore philosophical, as empirical. In *The Conflict of the Faculties*, Kant insists that philosophy is based on reason, one of the main tenets of the Enlightenment, the 18th-century cultural turn which emphasized reason, empiricism, and domination of nature. These Enlightenment ideas replaced not only medieval superstitions about devils and witches, but also Renaissance humanism, and the fierce struggle for state and church power marked by the Glorious Revolution and the Civil War with Oliver Cromwell's Interregnum briefly displacing both the monarchy and traditional church hierarchy.

THE ENLIGHTENMENT PROJECT

The Enlightenment saw a monarchy reduced in power, and intellectual interest in a deity who viewed the world as a mechanism

DOI: 10.4324/9781032625744-6

set in motion and needing no further intervention (**Deism**). This is an entirely rational deity with a clockwork-like universe; therefore, persons of intellect and science could deduce the systems underlying nature and the universe, since the natural world was mechanistically organized. John Locke's empiricism and Rene Descartes's rationalism are often taken as starting points for the emphasis on logical thought in all fields, from politics to chemistry. Those working with Enlightenment premises included French philosophers and encyclopedists, whose combined efforts produced encyclopedias of knowledge that documented what was known and being discovered about the world. The political philosopher William Godwin, Mary Shelley's father, for instance, studied under Abraham Rees, who wrote the *Cyclopaedia, or an Universal Dictionary of Arts and Sciences* (1728–1751). These thinkers included Scottish philosophers and scientists who specialized in empiricism. Similar developments led to the modernization of the German university. And in Germany's Romantic period, beginning with Kant's research, philosophy focused on how the mind thinks, the premise being that the mind's workings could also be deduced logically as a scientific endeavor. German philosophers like Hegel who followed Kant viewed philosophy *as* science itself; natural science still entwine speculative thought (philosophy) and empirical research (what we term 'science').

In the heady atmosphere of the Enlightenment, when it seemed human endeavor could finally control natural forces and parse the secrets of nature, the embodied past of the earth, and the human body, mechanics was of as much interest as the hard sciences. Industrialization meant that innovations in manufacture were supremely important for capitalist societies such as Britain's. The middling classes as well as leisured upper classes participated in experimental work, whether to improve the production of pottery as Josiah Wedgwood did, or to engage in lab science as the chemist Humphry Davy did. The creation of numerous Royal Societies in England, designed to stimulate discovery, were places where new knowledge could be shared, debated, and disproved. The academic society extended to colonial knowledge with the investigation of other cultures and languages as in the Royal Asiatic Society of Bengal, and later with Asiatic societies founded in England and Ireland. In France it was the Royal Academies;

in Scotland and Germany, the universities. In nearly all cases, the new knowledge was thought to help in understanding not just the present, but also the past, and therefore to help shape the future.

Not surprisingly then, the Enlightenment began the revival of historiography with Edward Gibbons's masterly history of the Roman Empire; the Romantic period followed his lead as history became, along with biography and **travel writing**, much more popular than fiction and poetry among the reading public. It was novelists and poets who began to write about the future in ways that foresaw the limits of human scientific endeavor; the most famous example of this dark vision of future scientific progress is Mary Shelley's *Frankenstein*. But for the most part, science and manufacturing predicted a bright and prosperous future, one that would make amends for the devastations of revolution and the Napoleonic Wars. Historiography as a field of literary endeavor was aligned with the creation of encyclopedias as a necessary way to systematically organize knowledge: France's *Encyclopédie*, a "Systematic Dictionary of the Sciences, Arts and Crafts," and Britain's *Encyclopedia Britannica* are perhaps the best known today, but German philosophers such as Hegel and Novalis were engaged in producing encyclopedias of natural philosophy and other encyclopedia projects were being devised.

Part of the historical project was not just the history of cultures, monarchical reigns, and individual lives, but also the history of the earth. The accurate dating of the earth's creation was hotly debated, since insisting on dates that do not accord with biblical record leaned toward heresy. Geology became a pastime for amateurs and a pursuit for those more scientifically inclined. Geological strata were producing evidence of prehuman life, including dinosaur fossils, challenging the biblical narrative. This challenged how people thought about the past and contributed to the mode begun earlier in the 18th century of ruminating on remains, whether in graveyards or among antiquities. These interests combined in the new field of archaeology, which focused on the antiquities of Rome, Greece, and Egypt. Associated with geology and archaeology was a more speculative endeavor of comparative history, in which determining the oldest civilizations (China's was determined to be older than India's, and so forth) went hand in hand with the field of art history founded by the

Hellenist Johann Joachim Wincklemann. These topics were neither discrete nor segregated in the period but were interconnected through their deep dives into what had been previously unrecognized or unseen, revealing new depths in what can be known.

HISTORY AS KNOWLEDGE AND POSSESSION

Historiography was integrally linked with colonialism and empire. The history of India was written by men working for the East India Company who were founding members of the Royal Asiatic Society of Bengal. "**World geographies**" were written to make sense of what was being learned about the Americas, Asia, the Balkans, and further abroad, spurred by improvements in cartography, which produced new atlases. And travel writing by both eminent persons with political or military expertise, as well as by first-time authors, was extremely popular. History itself became ground for colonizing; narratives are inherently subjective and biased (one need only look to Shakespeare's history plays to see the Tudor bias), and historiography is the art of historical narration. Sir Walter Scott must have recognized this when he decided to write the history of the Jacobite rebellion as a novel, *Waverley; Or, 'Tis Sixty Years Since* (1814), producing the first historical novel. The genre became one of the most popular in the period, with women increasingly trying their hand at it. But history, too, became extremely popular as the scientific eye turned toward it as an area of knowledge acquisition. One of the most successful historians was also a woman: the Whig historian Catharine Macaulay published her eight-volume *The History of England from the Accession of James I to the Revolution* (1778–1783) to critical acclaim, going from an unpublished author to "the Celebrated Mrs. Macaulay" immediately after the first volume was published (Hill 16). Her success was based on making history compelling reading. But fact and fiction, history and historical novels, had blurred: writers on history and historical figures such as Godwin, who published *Sketches of History* (1784), *History of the Commonwealth* (1824–1828), and several historical biographies, also wrote about the history of science in *Lives of the Necromancers* (1834). Writers immersed in history such as Anna Barbauld, Percy

Shelley, and Mary Shelley (especially her historical novel *Valperga*) were also deeply concerned with futurity, as in Barbauld's poem "Eighteen-Hundred and Eleven," Percy Shelley's play *The Cenci*, and Mary Shelley's novel *The Last Man*. And the future had much to do with the growth and strength of the British empire and its relations with its colonies.

One of the clearest examples of the connection between writing, history, and colonialism is the East India Company, through which writers such as Charles Lamb found a job as clerk, which spurred his interests in the Company's imports, and philologists (historical linguists) like Sir William Jones, who found the history of India more compelling than the work he was employed to do. Jones, who moved to Bengal to serve as a judge, translated ancient sacred texts and wrote a history of India, and to promote his research he founded the first Asiatic Society. The stretch of the East India Company was immense, and despite the intellectual resources one could glean from it as by-products, it was primarily an engine of empire. By the late 1700s Britain already had a monopoly in the Indian provinces, with production of printed cotton fabrics and teas among its most lucrative exports. It also had a large army to enforce colonial submission, which was not always successful. The foothold in Asia this afforded allowed for a lucrative trade in porcelain, tea, and opium from China, which first had to be wrested from the Portuguese in a lengthy power struggle (Puga 71–6). Because traders were only allowed at certain ports the history and cartography of China had to be based on journals of political emissaries such as Lord Macartney, mentioned in Jane Austen's *Mansfield Park*.

But the history of Britain could be pursued at home. Roman Britain could begin to be parsed from the local discoveries of antiquarians (the genteel forerunners of archaeologists), while the historical aspects of Scotland, Wales, Cornwall, and Ireland gained interest particularly in literary works that praised the ancient role of the Welsh bard and bemoaned the results of the Enclosure Acts that drove peasants from ancestral lands. Thomas Gray's 18th century "The Bard. A Pindaric Ode" (1757) was inspired by his research in medieval history; it in turn inspired Romantic poets to take up the theme as well as Scott, who used his historical research for his hugely popular poems about Scottish history before turning to writing historical novels. The Enclosure Acts were disastrous for Scotland, and William Wordsworth's lyric "The Solitary Reaper" (1807) recounts this from an experience he had while traveling to Scotland with his sister Dorothy in 1803. Scotland was another "unknown" territory where travel and travel writing began in the 18th century as a form of knowing the world, popularized in James Boswell's journal account of his travels there with Samuel Johnson. The world began near at hand, since traveling began to be something that those not belonging to the upper classes could enjoy. But more adventurous travelers, including several women, published accounts of travels to the Near East and Egypt, and the West Indies. There were also the maritime accounts of famous exploratory voyages such as those of Captain James Cook. Cook took three voyages to the Pacific, mapping previously uncharted coastlines from Easter Island to Hawaii and Alaska, claiming territory for the British crown, and encountering peoples of the Pacific isles. Literature was directly inspired by such accounts: although Coleridge was highly influenced by George Shelvocke's *A Voyage Around the World by Way of the Great South Sea* (1726) in his "Rime of the Ancient Mariner," the poem is more generally based on the scientific and medical information in Cook's accounts of his voyages. *Frankenstein* begins with the frame story of the scientifically minded Captain Walton, who in endeavoring to find the North Pole is emulating famous explorers like Cook. Cook's voyages inspired actual polar explorers who were seeking both geographical and historical knowledge, in the sense that the poles could also explain something about the earth's history. And, as for Cook, the first to discover a pole could also claim it for their nation: geographical, historical, and scientific knowledge were indeed a form of possession that translated in many cases into geopolitical power.

SCIENCE AS POWER: *FRANKENSTEIN* AS HISTORY, AS SCIENCE, AS FUTURITY

If William Godwin's stab at science was through the biographies of medieval alchemists in *Lives of the Necromancers*, his daughter

Mary Shelley took a more avid interest, inspired by Percy Shelley's own university experiments in chemistry and his curiosity about experimentation with electricity and magnetism. Scientifically minded gentlemen in the 18th century experimented endlessly with how to harness electricity from electrical storms. Benjamin Franklin famously did it with kites while the Shelleys were fascinated, as were so many others, by the Italian physician and physicist Luigi Galvani's experiments in 1791 with electrical stimulation of dead frogs' legs. Although such scientific breakthroughs coexisted with theories of galvanism, magnetism, spontaneous combustion of the body, spontaneous generation, and other pseudoscientific theories, Galvani's experiments gave rise to the hope that electrical stimulation could be used medically, and, even today, electrical stimulation of the brain is still used for psychiatric maladies. But harnessing this natural force required the multiple innovations in batteries that could functionally work.

The battery is one of the lesser-known miracles of the age. Like locomotives, which also were invented at this time, batteries were not imaginatively stimulating, but it was through them that electricity could move from being a natural phenomenon only to being a tool for human use.

In the 1790s, Galvani and his friend Alessandro Volta, who also conducted experiments with electricity, together worked on the theory that when two different metals were connected by a third wet object, electricity could be generated. In 1800, Volta invented the first battery capable of generating energy chemically and storing that energy. This and subsequent innovations in the battery by other scientists were large objects, hardly practicable for actual use. The liquid medium meant that they could leak and short circuit. The first battery without these and other problems was invented in 1835 by the Scottish William Cruickshank.

One pseudoscientific theory that enjoyed a tremendous fad due to its supposed healthful benefits employed a combination of electrical stimulation (and batteries) with magnets for sex therapy. It was proposed and employed by the Scottish entrepreneur James Graham, and he put his theory into practice in "Temples of Health," with the first one built in the middle of fashionable London. Here wealthy patrons were treated in the "Celestial

Bed," given electromagnetic treatments as well as ones using **pneumatic chemistry**, and sold questionable medicines. He also employed beautiful young women to model their perfect bodies: one such "Goddess of Health" was Emma Hart, who while still in her twenties was famously to become the wife of the wealthy Sir William Hamilton, British ambassador to the Kingdom of Naples. Lady Emma Hamilton's rise to the upper classes gave middle-class young women hope (one thinks of Jane Austen's *Pride and Prejudice*, in which the heroine Elizabeth Bennet marries the aristocratic Mr. Darcy), and matched the plots of romance novels generally. By contrast, Graham provided material for satirical literature, from plays, satires, poems, and newspaper pieces. Pseudoscience, like alchemy, was ripe for the literary imagination whereas hard science was more difficult to cultivate.

In *Frankenstein*, with its combination of science, exploration, anxiety over history (particularly the survival of family), and a future threatened by an experiment gone wrong, the young not-yet married Mary Godwin produced the first work of science fiction. Her debut novel, unsigned and attributed to Percy Shelley at first, innovated the melding of scientific experimentation and literary treatment, an invention that remains one of the most popular genres of fiction read today.

Frankenstein brings together history (alchemy; peasant/lord relations), science, nature, and futurity (the death of humankind, foreshadowing her predictive novel *The Last Man*). Excluding the frame narrative involving Captain Walton and his voyage of exploration, the novel initially resembles one written by Mary Godwin's father, *St. Leon: A Tale of the Sixteenth Century* (1799). A historical romance that anticipates Sir Walter Scott's more realistic historical novels, *St. Leon* tells the story of a young aristocrat who is unwillingly inducted into the magical science of alchemy. Learning how to make gold out of base metals and the secret of immortal life at first seem the way to resolve the crushing debts to which St. Leon's gambling addiction has reduced his wife and small children. But both turn out to be terrible curses: the inexplicable resources of gold cause suspicion wherever he moves to, and his unchanging body – which makes him outlive all those he loves – arouses the direst suspicions, eventually causing him to become a victim of the Inquisition. This theme of scientific miracles that curse rather than bless is the primary concern of Shelley's novel.

In her novel, Victor Frankenstein seeks to create an immortal being so that disease will no longer ravage humanity, particularly loved ones such as his mother whose early death inspired his frenzied research. The reader is warned early on that this experiment will go wrong, and not just by the frame narrative in which a young Captain Walton encounters a nearly dead Victor, aged beyond his years, the very opposite of St. Leon except in the disaster caused by meddling with the laws of nature. We are also given a strong clue in Victor's history as he relates it to Walton: his father possessed books by the preeminent alchemists such as Paracelsus, which Victor was allowed to read. The fault with these earlier authors was, as Victor's university professors explained, "exploded science," but also and more important to the novel's framing ideas, that great alchemists like Paracelsus sought not the philosopher's stone and the elixir of life, but rather to create a universal knowledge. This knowledge could not be found in books but only through wide experience of the world and nature: he sought a way to understand all things. As the novel's subtitle indicates ("The Modern Prometheus"), the problem with Promethean desire, alchemy, and modern science – such as Paracelsus demonstrated – is their combined assault on the divide between creator and creation. The challenge of *Frankenstein* is precisely that which Victor's creation throws at him: what happens when nature resents this and fights back?

Victor's account of the lab science and innovations he employed to make his creature are necessarily blurred over in the novel: Shelley is imagining what might happen, but she is using contemporary science to do so. Anatomists had already sketched the body's nervous, circulatory, muscular, and skeletal systems. Electricity had been used to stimulate dead matter; the elements of the air we breathe had been isolated; advances in theories of blood and its circulation were made. All these discoveries were available in printed lectures and treatises for the amateur to read. In the section on disease in *Zoonomia: Or, the Laws of Organic Life*, for instance, Erasmus Darwin (grandfather of Charles Darwin) had already proposed the innate nature of emotions, the vices (including pride of family, ambition – both of which apply to Victor – rage, and hate, which apply to the creature), the will, voluntary folly, and insanity. By systematically organizing various illnesses, Darwin puts forth the idea that these, which Victor intended to eradicate by making an immortal, perfect being, are the unavoidable condition of the created. Perfection, in other words, is not what science is good at.

But what science *was* good at in the period, and what Victor's wild experiment illustrates well, is that with all the developments in scientific understanding and instruments, reimagining what matter is, what it is capable of, and what it can be transformed into, was now possible. The alchemical dream was becoming the scientific reality. As Richard Sha explains,

> In the Romantic period, matter is increasingly understood in terms of dynamism—force and affinity—and what this means is that change and motion become inevitable. The problem now becomes how to measure human change against the forces of the world.
>
> (37)

Electromagnetism, hydraulics, optics and color theory, and isolation of gases, and early theories of evolution (developed from comparative study of species and geological fossil theory) all combined to produce an understanding of how inanimate elements and forces are what compose animate matter. Life is dynamic and the life force is discoverable.

How science had reached the point at which Mary Shelley could mine it for her dystopian science fiction is an interesting history, for the preceding decades had been ones of enormous strides in the sciences, instruments, machinery, and engines. The next section begins to detail how innovations and discoveries were being made, from businessmen to the university-educated.

THE MICRO AND MACRO ASPECTS OF SCIENCE

Earlier 18th-century scientific societies in which inventors shared their experiments shaped scientific culture. Much of this work was done by innovative industrialists such as Josiah Wedgwood, who needed a better way to determine a kiln's temperature to perfect the firing of his pottery in his model factory, Etruria. His contributions to the **Lunar Society of Birmingham**, part of the Midlands Enlightenment (an arising of experimentation and circulation of ideas derived from the Scottish Enlightenment, which specialized in empiricism) were not unique; this was a regular gathering of men whose experiments had practical ends, where new discoveries could be reported and the results shared. Unlike the **Royal Society** and **Royal Institution**, both under royal charter, the five men of the Lunar Society were of the middling classes, but their aims were practical rather than academic so that their inventions had lasting effects: Wedgwood, Matthew Boulton and James Watt, Erasmus Darwin, and Joseph Priestley. It is this group I will focus on for its remarkable discoveries.

Wedgwood was a remarkable man who decided he would use his background in stoneware to make pottery that could compete with the porcelain imported from China. British pottery was heavy and coarse in comparison with the delicacy of porcelain. Wedgwood's first real innovation was "creamware," a beautiful style of pottery that made him potter to the Queen; her patronage in turn granted creamware the name "Queen's ware." Wedgwood expanded his designs into more lines including "jasperware," which had an unglazed matte finish that made it stand out from ordinary pottery. Characteristically pale blue, he used this method to imitate ancient Greek urns and similar objects, which made it important for those decorating their homes in the "**Grecian**" mode, made popular through Sir Hamilton's sale to the new British Museum of his antique vase collection (and the publication of detailed engravings of the Grecian urns and other objects in 1766–1767), and architecturally perfected through the designs of Robert and James Adams. In order to perfect his pottery, Wedgwood needed a way to determine the internal temperature of his kilns; mercury thermometers burst in the high heat necessary to fire ceramics. Working with what was already available, he invented a more reliable pyrometer; although it was not a thermometer, it was a good substitute and was not bested for at least two decades.

Another member of the Lunar Society, Erasmus Darwin, was intimately connected with the Wedgwoods, and through the intermarriage of their two families Charles Darwin was the grandson of both Erasmus and Josiah Wedgwood. Erasmus Darwin became renowned for his botanical studies, but like many scientists of the period he was engaged in many different pursuits. A physician, Darwin was also engaged in natural philosophy – most specifically plant life – physiology, and poetry. Like many men actively engaged with the ideas of the time, Darwin was a Freemason, which introduced him to the idea of the interconnectedness of all life, and to the freedom of the individual. These ideas connected to his abolitionism and to his theories on evolution, predating those of his famous grandson. Like the other members of the Lunar Society, he was also an inventor. In 1761, he was elected to the Royal Society; he also belonged to the Derby Philosophical Society, another influential group of the Midlands Enlightenment. And by 1792, his work was recognized by his election to the American Philosophical Society in Philadelphia.

Darwin is best remembered for his epic poems that transformed botany into entertaining but educational reading. He began by forming a botanical society at Lichfield, where the poet Anna Seward immortalized many of the celebrated persons living there. **The Botanical Society**'s task was to translate the works of Carl Linnaeus from Latin into English, a project that took years to complete. Two of Darwin's subsequent poems – *Loves of the Plants* and *Economy of Vegetation*, both also published together as *The Botanic Garden* (all published in 1791) – taught Linnaeus's system to the reading public. Shocking in its day, *The Botanic Garden* presents flowers as sexed, using an allegory of plant love with male stamens and female pistils to transform flowers into marital couples. William Blake often depicted anthropomorphized flowers as sexual beings in his poems of the 1790s in ways reminiscent of Darwin's conception.

Darwin's most important works, however, are *Zoonomia* (1794–1796) and *Temple of Nature* (1803). In *Zoonomia*, Darwin reveals his work as a physiologist, including there an important chapter on pathology and another on propagation that anticipates later work on evolution, a theme that he refines in *Temple of Nature*, whose title derives from ideas circulating in Masonic circles, but which presents his most refined conception of evolution. In the poem, he traces the development of life from the microorganism to the human being to human society. Although Darwin's poetry is didactic and meant to popularize rather than innovate artistically, his works influenced many poets of the day from Seward to Wordsworth.

Another member of the Lunar Society whose experiments influenced literature was the radical political theorist and chemist Joseph Priestley. His experiments with oxygen, which he isolated independently of other discoveries of the gas in 1774, are the subject of Anna Laetitia Barbauld's poem "The Mouse's Petition," which depicts the experimental animal's suffering during the experiment. However, she excuses him with a note appended to the poem's title:

> * To Doctor PRIESTLEY.
>
> The Author is concerned to find, that what was intended as the petition of mercy against justice, has been construed as the plea of humanity against cruelty. She is certain that cruelty could never be apprehended from the Gentleman to whom this is addressed; and the poor animal would have suffered more as the victim of domestic economy, than of philosophical curiosity.
>
> (38)

Priestley also invented carbonated water and discovered several gases, and wrote a *History and Present State of Electricity* (1767) and *Optics (The History and Present State of Discoveries Relating to Vision, Light and Colours)* (1772). Optics was of international interest, with Goethe also writing on the subject of optics and color. Barbauld became friendly with Priestley when in 1761 he moved to Warrington as a tutor at the Warrington Dissenting Academy, where Barbauld's father had also taught. There Priestley joined the circle that included Anna, her brother John Aikin, a well-known physician, and Josiah Wedgwood.

Priestley was more widely known, however, for his radical theology. A Unitarian, he believed that human progress was deeply tied to necessitarianism and to the natural world. In *Institutes of Natural and Revealed Religion* (1772–1774) he argued that experience of the Divine must match one's experience in the natural world, thereby bridging the scientific and theological elements of his thinking. He also argued for **Socinianism**, materialism, and determinism, and later was a proponent in favor of both the American War for Independence and the French Revolution. His political and theological radicalism made Priestley an object of violent attack, and after a mob burned down his Birmingham home and church, he fled to London and then to America, where he lived out the last decade of his life.

Two other influential members of the Lunar Society were Matthew Boulton and his partner James Watt. The original five members frequently met in Darwin's home and Boulton's. Like the other members, Boulton was multi-faceted: he was an inventor, mechanical engineer, and silversmith. His business partner was the Scotsman James Watt, the engineer who invented the Watt steam engine. When Boulton became Watt's partner, he applied his business acumen learned at his father's manufactory of small metal objects and toys to what became known as the Boulton & Watt steam engine. Their engines allowed mines and factories to be mechanized, as well as mills formerly depending on water power. Boulton also invented an improvement to coin minting, making the copper penny unforgeable, and later greatly increased the Royal Mint's capacity for production of coins. He also invented many improvements in the manufacture of small metal objects such as buckles and buttons, essential to the clothing industry. The first of these was when he was 17 years old and invented a way to inlay enamel in silver buckles that were hugely popular in both Britain and France. His manufactory also produced silver-hilt swords, another fashion accessory.

The steam engine propelled the Industrial Revolution, but importantly for the Romantic age when the circulation of materials and goods was required for the increasing pace of consumerism, it propelled the innovations necessary for the first successful locomotive. The first was built in Shropshire by Richard Trevithick in 1802 for the ironworks there. Two years later, one of Trevithick's locomotives made the first successful rail journey in South Wales, again for an ironworks company. George Stephenson built his locomotive for the first public steam railway in the world, the Stockton & Darlington Railway, and in 1829, his son Robert built a locomotive improved for speed, The Rocket, which led to their company producing steam trains for Britain, the United States, and much of the Continent. In 1830, Stephenson opened the Liverpool & Manchester Railway, built for passenger and goods trains; it started the revolution in making travel to other parts of Britain economically available to the middling classes, a phenomenon lovers of nature such as William Wordsworth decried bitterly as his beloved Lake Windermere in the Lake District became a tourist destination for those escaping the heat of southern England when the Kendal and Windermere Railway established a train station by the lake's shore.

Inventors and scientists were as engaged with nature as poets, and as interested in production as businessmen, although for knowledge rather than profit. Two improvements in viewing nature were integral to the period: the microscope and the telescope. Innovations in lens grinding in the 17th century had led to microscopes being capable of magnifying microbial life; by the Romantic period, microscopes were instruments with fluid-filled chambers that led to increasing discoveries in investigations in both the medical and natural history fields. These discoveries led to the emergence of new scientific specializations, particularly biological disciplines. The term "natural philosophy" began to be replaced by "chemistry," "physics," "botany," and "zoology," while "natural science" became known as "geology." The microscope was particularly useful in transforming botany. Studies of pond water revealed microscopic life forms that did not fit neatly into established taxonomies, for instance. Alexander von Humboldt's research during his wide-ranging travels in the last half of the 18th century established the relationship between species and their environment, but the microscope helped deepen knowledge of the species themselves and their differences.

The impact of botany, and, therefore, biology on modern science can best be understood, through the advances in microscope lenses, by theories of the cell as the basic unit of the organism, a theory which was led by German botanist Mattias Jakob Schleiden along with his fellow scientists Theodor Schwann and Rudolf Virchow in 1838. But even before that, philosophers such as Hegel and British physicians were describing microscopic bodies that were the basic elements of all organisms. Already by 1831, however, Robert Brown had discovered the cell nucleus, using the microscopes of the period before the more improved staining methods of the later 19th century were introduced.

Beyond microscopy, the field of botany in particular had developed as a cultural as well as scientific interest. Specimens were collected on scientific voyages as well as on trips made to the interiors of the New World and elsewhere globally, as in Humboldt's explorations. Botanical specimens were not just brought to royal and university gardens: cities started their own gardens, such as London's Chelsea Gardens. And the rich wanted rare specimens in gardens of their own. As with the art of floral still life, made popular even before the Dutch tulip craze, botanical specimens needed to be illustrated before they perished, and at different stages of the life cycle. Middling and upper-class women were taught watercolor as one of the arts taught at finishing schools or at home and could apply their skills not just to painting sketches of nature, but to plant specimens, flowers, and insects. Some became quite expert at botanical illustration, earning reputations as botanical illustrators for publications. Among them were Elizabeth Blackwell, who published her own botanical art in bi-weekly supplements as *Curious Herbal*; Rachel Ruysch, who made a long career in flower painting; and Françoise Basseporte, who became botanical illustrator to the king. Mary Delany innovated on the art by making her exquisite botanical illustrations out of cut paper.

Part of the cultural interest in botany had begun with royal and university botanical gardens that, as with the case of Kew Gardens, became popular visiting places to stroll and investigate specimens brought from around the world. One of the principal promoters of research voyages and specimen collection was Sir Joseph Banks, whose personal collection outgrew his house to such an extent that he donated it to the nation to form the basis of Britain's natural history museum. Banks obtained his specimens from explorations such as those of Captain Cook, on whose first voyage he had served as the mission's botanist, and from the Macartney Mission to China, of which he was a principal proponent as President of the Royal Society. He had been growing tea plants in his private gardens for nearly a decade when Cook's expedition to Tahiti took place in 1787; in need of new species of tea and other plants, he was a strong proponent of that mission as well. His ambition was to add global specimens to the Royal Botanic Gardens at Kew, although he also wanted to contribute new tea specimens to the Calcutta Botanical Garden (founded by an army officer of the East India Company also in 1787) (Thomas 165). Col. Robert Kyd, to produce commercially viable plants such as tea, teak, and East Indian spices grown in the gardens for Britain. Kyd also wanted to experiment with new specimens to help end the famine devastating the native population during the period, but like Banks, Kyd's principal concern was to correct what they both saw as a trade imbalance in tea with China; both wanted to see if tea could be grown commercially for Britain's use. (It was not until 1823 that a botanist discovered that Assam was already growing locally in India.) Therefore, in promoting the **Macartney Embassy**, one of Banks's chief aims was that among the plant specimens gathered that tea plants be particularly sought. Two men served as the embassy's botanical gardeners.

If Cook and Banks made botany and collection of specimens a mainstream interest, far expanded beyond the cabinets of curiosities of previous periods, Sir Humphry Davy made chemistry into a popular topic for lecture series as entertainment for amateurs and members of the public. Anne Lister, for instance, as far afield as Yorkshire, notes attending several chemistry lectures in Shibden as a young woman. Chemistry was the first real lab science, replacing the metaphysical understandings of nature such as alchemy, which was still being practiced in the 1700s, and more recent theories such as vitalism, which understood nature to work via fluids rather than chemicals. For instance, Aristotelian science understood fermentation (transformation associated with generation) and decay, or putrefaction, (transformation associated with death) as vital processes. But building on the work of the French chemist Antoine Lavoisier, whose work also pioneered important developments in biology, German scientists were creating the field of organic chemistry, producing an understanding of the interrelation of inorganic and organic matter. This is the basis of Victor Frankenstein's lab work while at the university, although he added the energy of electricity to stimulate the interaction of the two. It was Davy who pioneered the technique of separating elements using electricity, beginning with potassium and sodium, providing more inspiration for Shelley. Davy's specific form of chemistry became that of electrochemistry. As a young man Davy discovered that nitrous oxide, or laughing gas, could provide anesthetic relief, and it was the first anesthetic available for physicians and surgeons. Eventually Davy's discoveries gained him honors such as: President of the Royal Society, Member of the Royal Irish Academy, a Fellow of the Geological Society of London, and a member of the American Philosophical Society.

Scientists working in organic chemistry such as Friedrich Wöhler and Justus Liebig began to be able to create organic substances in the lab by combining chemicals (Jackson 138–60). By not involving a living organism, these chemists challenged the theory of vitalism. Along with organic chemistry came the rise of experiments in physiology, another link with Mary Shelley's novel. The popularity of books and lectures on chemistry, especially Davy's 1806 "On Some Chemical Agencies of Electricity," reveals how influential this new science was. Davy's membership in different scientific societies similar to the Birmingham Lunar Society reveals that innovation and widespread interest were the guiding principles of the Romantic age; knowledge was not the concern of a few elites but a widespread ambition. The connections between lab chemistry and geology were evident enough to Davy that he helped found the Geological Society in much the same spirit as Sir Joseph Banks helped found the Macartney Embassy. Evident too is how information connected the West, from Germany to North America, as much as trade did; the circulation of knowledge and power was an element of the same phenomenon that characterized the age.

The emerging discipline of geology, like the other new sciences, also brought natural history and natural philosophy closer together. The establishment of strata or layered deposits of earth that contained fossilized remains of organisms, discoverable in the coastal cliffs for instance, and immortalized in Charlotte Smith's masterful poem "Beachy Head" (1807). Although she integrates a romantic story of loss into it, as well as national history with the invasions of the seafaring Vikings and channel-crossing Normans, the poem contains significant sections on the remains of past geological ages as revealed in the strata visible at the cliff's edge, although she doubts scientists could accurately trace the history revealed in them:

> What time these fossil shells,
> Buoy'd on their native element, were thrown
> Among the imbedding calx: when the huge hill
> Its giant bulk heaved, and in strange ferment
> Grew up a guardian barrier, 'twixt the sea
> And the green level of the sylvan weald.
> Ah! very vain is Science' proudest boast,
> And but a little light its flame yet lends
> To its most ardent votaries; since from whence
> These fossil forms are seen, is but conjecture ...
>
> *(384–93)*

What Smith doubted was that geologists could use the strata to link the spatial distribution of organisms to their chronological period. The keen interest in doing so was a necessary step in concepts of evolution, since some fossils were discovered to be previously unknown species rather than the calcified seashell fossils Smith was writing about.

At the same time, the naturalist Georges Cuvier, who focused on zoology, was also working in comparative anatomy, a field that had important developments for the developing science of paleontology. By comparing contemporary species with fossils of mammals, Cuvier could prove that species could become extinct. Previously, fossils were believed to be of species still living in other parts of the globe. The evidence of species extinction in a period of devastating revolution and war led inevitably to poetic meditations on the ruins of empire, as in Barbauld's dark poem "Eighteen Hundred and Eleven," her 1812 meditation on the ruins of civilization as reflected in the shocks of the Napoleonic Wars. In it she envisions an abandoned London, ruined from war and as melancholic a prospect as the remains of Ancient Egypt, a reminder of what can befall a people – and the individual – when war and power outweigh art and culture.

Geology led to both natural history with paleontology and human history with archaeology. Pompeii and Herculaneum had been discovered earlier in the 18th century; well-preserved evidence of ancient Roman life helped turn the gentleman antiquarian into a scientifically minded archaeologist. But the process was not that smooth: ancient remains continued to be valued more for their aesthetic value than for the scientific knowledge they provided. As with Sir William Hamilton's Roman vases, other archaeological work was conducted as a kind of spoils of war. Napoleon's Egyptian Campaign, designed to frustrate British trade routes and to gain control over the overland Silk Trade Route, was equally a scientific mission to measure, sketch, and bring home Egyptian antiquities. The British capture of French warships loaded with Egyptian art and statuary made the Egyptian collection in the new **British Museum** possible. Likewise, when the engineer and entrepreneur Giovanni Belzoni traveled to Egypt to offer his services in solving Pasha Ali's problems with irrigation beyond the banks of the Nile to the pyramids with a hydraulic machine he had invented, he found a better use of his engineering skills. He was the first to enter one of the great Giza pyramids as well as the tomb of Seti I in the Valley of the Kings. Through engineering feats and his own enormous strength, Belzoni removed large monuments of the ancient Egyptian culture, including an enormous bust of Ramesses II, and shipped them back to London in the hopes of profit.

HISTORY, SCIENCE, AND THE FUTURE

Archaeology, which marries history and science but can give insights on the future, was the scientific counterpart of the 18th-century genre of meditations on ruins. A quintessential text of that genre, Volney's 1791 *Ruins of Empire*, gave the genre a more political, future-oriented element. It was a work so widely read that the *Ruins* not only helped propel the French Revolution's civic-mindedness but also inspired Napoleon in his world-empire ambitions. Volney's meditation on ancient empires was itself motivated by his travels through Syria and Egypt, two lands already proven archaeological treasure troves, which he published as *Travels in Syria and Egypt, During the Years 1783, 1784, & 1785* (London 1788).

Meditations on ancient ruins, in fact, are already necessarily inflected with anxieties about the future. As the Napoleonic wars devastated increasing swathes of Europe, and the numbers of dead soldiers outweighed political gains for many at home, these worries became more real. Added to this was a year of changed climate and poor harvests due to the atmospheric effects in 1816 from an eruption the previous year of the Indonesian volcano Mount Tambora. The "**year without a summer**," 1816 led to imaginings of dystopian futures. Thus, the earth and nature were not the only objects scientists and amateurs aimed at: the heavens, including how the atmosphere was affected by changed conditions, were also fair game, and investigation of them became increasingly possible through advances in telescopes and experiments with air, and they became part of the imaginative terrain as well.

Mary Shelley combined all these aspects of a world in which the future looked dark both phenomenally and politically in her novel *The Last Man*. This work imagines a future in which humanity comes to an end due to a plague that cannot be escaped. With a biblical nod to the past, the plague originates in Egypt in the Nile mud. Its ferocity causes the most rational schemes of a newly democratic community to go awry, and the devastation of disease and starvation on families and communities is illustrated in terms of the emotional toll on individual characters. But the novel is also intriguingly set in the future world of the 21st century – our own. Telescopes play a part, as does the most advanced air travel of Shelley's day, the hot air balloon. Her idea of balloon travel foreshadows travel by blimps in the early 20th century and was used during World War I.

Hot air balloons were the vogue beginning in the late 1700s when several Frenchmen successfully experimented with modern balloon travel. The first manned balloon flight was performed in 1783 by Jean-François Pilâtre de Rozier with a tethered flight from the yard of the Reveillon workshop in the Faubourg Saint-Antoine, with the first free manned flight occurring a few weeks afterward by Pilâtre de Rozier and Marquis François d'Arlandes. The French also used a hot air balloon for military observation in 1794. Mary Shelley imagined a future in which balloons functioned like blimps, providing air travel whose speed far exceeded that of horse-drawn carriages, making lengthy or intercontinental trips more expedient.

Advances in telescopes were another scientific achievement that had a deep impact on the cultural imagination. Although shorter, functional telescopes such as those used on ships were commercially available for the public by 1758, the astronomical telescope that required an observatory became an object of public interest through the small astronomical and terrestrial magnetic observatory built for George III at Kew, where the royal botanical gardens are. The king made his astronomical observations with a Short's reflecting telescope, with which he was able to view the transit of Venus in 1769. Even more popular was the work of William Herschel, a music teacher in Bath who experimented with reflector telescope mirrors. In 1778, Herschel built a seven-foot focal length telescope using his mirrors. As he became more interested in astronomy, he innovated on his telescope several times, and in 1789, his largest reflecting telescope was finished, a 40-foot telescope which he installed at his house in Slough; for 50 years it was the largest telescope in the world. One of his most important discoveries was that of Enceladus, Saturn's sixth moon, and Mimas, the seventh (North 437–42).

Herschel collaborated with his sister and fellow astronomer Caroline Herschel, who discovered several comets, including the periodic comet 35P/Herschel–Rigollet. Another famous woman astronomer was the American Maria Mitchell, known for discovering a comet in 1847. She was the first woman to be a professional astronomer and the first to be a professor of astronomy. She traveled to Europe and Britain, visiting observatories, including that of the Herschels. The family she traveled with for part of her tour was that of Nathaniel Hawthorne. And it was she who taught her friend Ralph Waldo Emerson to use a telescope. Thus the worlds of literary imagination, scientific inquiry, historical imagination, and futuristic speculation collide in Romantic period culture and the cultural imagination of that era.

SUMMARY

During the period, scientific knowledge was reorganized from philosophical categories to modern ones. The modernization of Scottish and German universities drove this intellectual focus on scientific pursuits, whether pure or practical science.

- The 18th-century encyclopedia projects undertaken by philosophers in France, Britain, Germany, and elsewhere channeled the drive to acquire new knowledge, new methods to attain it, and new mechanisms to put it to use.
- Knowledge acquisition was an imperial project both abroad and at home; the Royal Asiatic Society in Bengal as well as the Royal Society and Royal Institution in London had the throne behind them.
- Numerous domestic scientific societies were actively producing new models of scientific endeavor as well as mechanical innovations.
- History became another area for knowledge acquisition, and historiography became more scientifically oriented; however, history retained its narrative appeal, and historical novels were as popular as histories.

FURTHER READING

The Lunar Men by Uglow is an engaging discussion of some of the key innovators of the period and also gives a sense of how prevalent the spirit of localized scientific endeavor, both individual and collective, was. For the contributions of exceptional collectors to scientific knowledge, see O'Brian's *Joseph Banks*. The rapid advances in electrical energy can be surveyed in Pera's book on *Galvani and Volta*. The application of science to history is vividly portrayed in Giovanni Belzoni's exploits in unearthing Ancient Egyptian artifacts: see Mayes's *The Great Belzoni* and Hume's *Belzoni*. The impact the eruption of Mount Tambora on the Romantic imagination, reflected in *Frankenstein*, also had environmental and geological interest for the period. For the period's interest in the sky, see MacDonald's book on the Kew Observatory and Hoskin's book on William and Caroline Herschel. For more on Humphry Davy's contributions to science, see Knight. For the history of the East India Company and Royal Asiatic Society, their respective websites are good places to get a sense of the application of science to imperial concerns.

WEBSITES

The East India Company. https://www.nationaltrust.org.uk/discover/history/what-was-the-east-india-company.

The Royal Asiatic Society. https://royalasiaticsociety.org/about-us/.

WORKS CITED

Barbauld, nee Aikin, Anna Lætitia. "The Mouse's Petition." In *Poems*, 37–40. London: Printed for Joseph Johnson, 1773.

Behringer, Wolfgang. *Tambora and the Year without a Summer: How a Volcano Plunged the World into Crisis*. Cambridge: Polity, 2019.

Hill, Bridget. *The Republican Virago. The Life and Times of Catharine Macaulay, Historian*. Oxford: Clarendon Press, 1992.

Hoskin, Michael. *Discoverers of the Universe: William and Caroline Herschel*. Princeton: Princeton University Press, 2011.

Hume, Kvor Noël. *Belzoni: The Giant Archaeologists Love to Hate*. Charlottesville: University of Virginia Press, 2011.

Jackson, Catherine M. *Molecular World: Making Modern Chemistry*. Cambridge: MIT Press, 2023.

Knight, David. *Humphry Davy: Science and Power*. Cambridge: Cambridge University Press, 1992.

MacDonald, Lee T. *Kew Observatory and the Evolution of Victorian Science, 1840–1910*. Pittsburgh: University of Pittsburgh Press, 2018.

Mayes, Stanley. *The Great Belzoni: The Circus Strongman Who Discovered Egypt's Treasures*. London: Tauris Parke, 2003.

North, John. *Cosmos: An Illustrated History of Astronomy and Cosmology*. Chicago: Chicago University Press, 2008.

O'Brian, Patrick. *Joseph Banks: A Life*. Chicago: University of Chicago Press, 1997.

Pera, Marcello. *The Ambiguous Frog: The Galvani-Volta Controversy on Animal Electricity*. Princeton: Princeton University Press, 1991.

Pilâtre de Rozier, Jean-François. *Première Expérience de la Montgolfière Construite Par Ordre Du Roi, Le 23 Juin 1774*. Vanves: Hachette Livre Bnf, 2013.

Puga, Rogério Miguel. *The British Presence in Macau, 1635–1793*. Hong Kong: Hong Kong University Press, 2013.

Sha, Richard C. *Imagination and Science in Romanticism*. Baltimore: Johns Hopkins University Press, 2018.

Smith, Charlotte. *Beachy Head: With Other Poems*. London, 1807.

Thomas, Adrian P. "The Establishment of Calcutta Botanic Garden: Plant Transfer, Science and the East India Company, 1786–1806." *Journal of the Royal Asiatic Society* 16, no. 2 (2006): 165–7.

Uglow, Jenny. *The Lunar Men: Five Friends Whose Curiosity Changed the World*. New York: Farrar, Straus and Giroux, 2002.

THE REGENCY

Social Life, Celebrity, and Literature

INTRODUCTION

Social life among the wealthy gains becomes exaggerated and excessive in the Regency, which was in some ways the high point of the Romantic period. The Regency combined Romantic era contradiction and ambition with spectacle and excess, but the next generation would reject these excesses in the tightening of social mores and manners dominated in the Victorian period. It was a period of lavish balls, expenditure, celebrity culture, and, in Britain, a blindness to the aftermath of the Napoleonic wars.

The Regency occupies an impressive amount of Western cultural space in the 21st century, with Jane Austen films, a resurgence of interest in Austen's life and the society about which she wrote (all of her novels were published within the Regency period), a fascination with Regency dress, and imaginative literary uses of the Regency, particularly the hugely successful series *Bridgerton* (2020–present). Although the Regency's resurgent popularity has renewed interest in the Romantic period generally, the nine-year period that constitutes the Regency – 1811–1820, the period in which the Prince of Wales served symbolically as Regent until the death of George III – was so much more. Although the individual, sensibility, and the human–nature relationship continued to be important, during the Regency, Britain leaned more heavily on global connections, humanitarian crises such as the slave trade, the effects of war on civilian populations, and on the philosophy of idealism. Important political work was being done toward the

DOI: 10.4324/9781032625744-7

emancipation of enslaved persons and on enlarging voting rights to include non-landowning men, termed "**Chartism**." And yet, at a time when the **Napoleonic Empire** was at its height in terms of wealth and conserving power, so too was the Regency a time of great excess but also political conservatism. Political radicals were being increasingly silenced whether through government harassment or through public sentiment turned against them. Women's rights seemed further away instead of nearer. Political idealists despaired of any real progressive gains for human rights. And yet, this was also when Chartism was on the rise and, in the years after the Regency, the Greeks would overthrow their Ottoman occupiers as a reminder that the democratic ideal was not dead. To comprehend the importance of the Regency, however, we first need to gain a greater understanding of social life generally during the period.

SOCIAL LIFE DURING THE ROMANTIC PERIOD

Social institutions of the period such as balls, spa towns, shopping arcades, and taking tea were where societal features such as excess and contradiction are highlighted. And the Prince of Wales set the tone; while he waited to become King George IV, as Regent he could at least be the cultural leader. His admiration for art and architecture, theater and music, fine dress and jewelry, fine cuisine, and magnificent parties gave the period an imprimatur that provides the fabric of our own reimagining of the period. The social life of the Regency was intensified in terms of consumerism and the spread of literary consumption, so that excess was a key marker of it. For instance, to be seen reading Byron's publications, whose works exemplify the Regency paradox of self-rumination and celebrity, conveyed a social mark of taste even if one didn't actually understand them – Byron instantiated excess. Another good example was the balls that typified the Romantic period generally but gained heightened importance in the Regency because they allowed individuals to make themselves a spectacle; the individual was put on display, and made of point of being so.

In terms of display, balls were designed specifically for those looking for a marriage partner, an increasingly difficult proposition during the Regency with the diminishment of available young men from the military engagements with France. Balls focused on showcasing girls between 16 and 18 for eligible young men to choose from, while unwed older adults of suitable income could also attend balls with an eye out for potential partners. Books such as *Mirror of Graces, or the English Lady's Costume* (anonymous, 1811) equated etiquette, comportment, or elegance, and dress for gentlewomen. However, this made girls and unwed adults vulnerable precisely because they were on display; they were open to vicious teasing by young men who "quizzed" their victim while pretending to assess her as if for sale, noting her weak points or publicly snubbing her for dances. However, for those young men serious about marriage, the Regency exhibited a growing shift from arranged marriages to conjugal or companionate marriages. Although marriages based on romantic love were more a fictional account than a reality, the shift toward conjugal marriages meant that partners tended to be chosen and approved by parents by social fit, whether the same social circles, university networks, or financial networks. This form of connection still gave women more agency than traditional arranged marriages, such as that of the Prince of Wales to Caroline of Brunswick; they met just prior to their wedding, and he detested her from the start. But even with the rise of conjugal marriages, novels pointed out the exclusionary nature of balls, the social valuation of women based on beauty rather than intelligence, and a focus on artifice at balls. Because of their increasing lavishness and frivolity, balls became a symbol of Regency excess, but because balls were also in contrast to romantic ideals of nature and philosophical concepts, they were a standing contradiction of the period.

Another important aspect of social life in the Romantic period was the **spa town**. Recognized for their healthful mineral water (for instance, Harrogate in North Yorkshire) or mineral salts (like Epsom in Surrey), spa towns became vacation spots for non-invalids where balls could also be attended. Two popular spas during the Romantic period were Tunbridge Wells in Kent, closer to London, and Bath. Both had become popular earlier, especially under the rule of Master of Ceremonies Beau Nash (1674–1762). Although spa towns were foremost used as health centers for those whose ailments were thought to benefit from daily bathing in mineral salts and drinking mineral water, Beau Nash was an important element in making both Bath and Tunbridge Wells attractive holiday sites as well.

Bath was revitalized during Nash's reign, and with its new town planning and architecture in the Georgian style, it became a desirable location to live as well. It benefited from speculative building, with the Circus becoming its best-known feature; this semi-circular array of townhouses was modeled on the Roman Colosseum and designed by Bath's most prominent architect John Wood, the Elder, and remains emblematic of the town. Nash was Master of Ceremonies for Bath from 1704 to 1761 and in 1735 also Master of Ceremonies for Tunbridge Wells. His domination of this function remained impactful through the Regency, although he was not himself what could be called a celebrity. Rather, he made it possible for others to be seen to be important. He was unique in innovating rules of civil behavior for visitors to Bath, which he posted in the Pump Room (where the mineral water could be drunk), insisting they behave as gentlemen and gentlewomen and thereby ushering in an era of manners that imitated to a degree the manners of civility practiced at court. One rule states "That no Gentleman or Lady take it ill that another Dances before them," while another maintains "That Gentlemen crowding before the Ladies at the Ball shew ill manners; and that none do so for the Future" (from the rules still posted at the Pump Room). These rules were designed to ensure good manners but at the same time Nash introduced a new informality so that social rank was not such a barrier to intercourse between aristocrats, gentry, and the rising middle ranks of society. Although his position was not official, Nash ruled Bath and later Tunbridge Wells: he regulated gambling (despite being addicted to gaming himself) by warning of cardsharps as well as compulsive gambling, and he was in charge of musicians playing at the balls in the assembly rooms. He matched young women with dancing partners and was even known to have a hand in marriage arrangements. Most importantly, he was the arbiter of which new arrivals to Bath would be admitted to the select society that represented the elite for the season. In this way, the rising middling classes could find their daughters dancing with sons of the gentry under the auspices of Nash himself. Although he had died before the Romantic period, his legacy was so well established that successive Masters of Ceremony continued his practice of facilitating the intermingling of social ranks, ensuring that young ladies had dance partners, and maintaining civil behavior at the concerts and gaming tables.

Bath enjoyed a renewed attractiveness for the Romantic era as it grew, with the new and elegant Upper Assembly Rooms, opened in 1771, replacing the original assembly rooms Nash presided over. The Upper Assembly Rooms, also built for balls, concerts, and gambling, boasted ten chandeliers of English lead crystal that at approximately three meters tall weighed between 150–200 kg each, and were equally expensive (Forsyth 91). Elegance was all. By 1801, Bath boasted over 40,000 inhabitants and was one of the largest cities in Britain (Forsyth 16). William Beckford moved to Bath in 1822, converting three houses into his residence in Lansdown Crescent.

Bath was not the only town revitalized by **Georgian architecture**. In 1825, toward the end of the Romantic period, London's new Regent Street in the West End was finished, but designs were begun in 1811, the year the Prince of Wales became Regent. Like the speculative buildings designed by John Wood the Elder in Bath, Regent Street is also an early example of town planning. Designed by architects John Nash and James Burton, it runs from just off Waterloo Place to Regent's Park, also named after the Prince of Wales. (Originally, it was meant to run from the Regent's Carlton House to the park [Fagan 7].) The street's centerpiece was a colonnaded shopping center where high-quality goods would rival those shops on nearby Bond Street. Its presence signaled the increased importance of consumerist culture in the Romantic period. As for visitors to Bath, shopping constituted a major entertainment along with balls, theater, and exhibitions.

Shopping arcades and shop emporiums would come to dominate major cities, and these created covered or indoor shopping centers where consumerism could be elevated to a fine art. Such spaces created a way for women to assert their character, their unique taste that could set them apart (Lynch 168). Shops and arcades created a public space for women at a time when the social space outside the home – where men debated politics, discussed business, made financial and political deals, and networked – was separate from the private sphere or domestic space that was proper to women of all classes. Middle- and upper-rank women were not supposed to leave the home unchaperoned. In *Pride and Prejudice*, Austen's heroine Elizabeth conducts solitary walks that earn her the condemnation of the Bingley sisters but the admiration of Mr. Darcy for her independence. This was an unusual response, however: more typical was the condemnation Anne Lister received for her solitary walks, which included not just local gossip but also sexual harassment from male laborers who considered her fair game since she was alone. But shopping was the one respectable activity outside the home women could pursue alone or with a female companion since the shop was a form of domestic space. Fabric and hat shops were associated with feminine concerns about dress, lace, ribbons, hats, and gloves, and made perfect places for conversation. Lynch's argument is that shops were acceptable places for women to go beyond gossip into discussions of recent events, the latest literary publications, political issues, and other subjects that normally were the province of men and that were not acceptable at the tea table. Milliners sold hats; haberdashers sold cloth, gloves, and hose; and dressmakers turned one's cloth and lace into gowns. All of these were also acceptable spaces for women of the trade classes to work in, providing an alternative to being a servant or agricultural worker. Shops, in other words, also allowed for increased opportunity, if not liberation.

Tea was the other activity that women dominated. Coffee shops were regarded as male spaces where politics and business discussions reigned; by contrast, tea was taken in the home and was often offered to visitors making afternoon social calls. It became an occasion for showing off elegant tea services, such as those made by Josiah Wedgwood's factory, and elegant manners. Elizabeth Kowaleski-Wallace has shown that certain tea services were designed to showcase the hostess's elegant hands, illustrating how tightly intertwined consumerism was with the body. And tea was considered a female entertainment. However, because tea was served in the home, it meant the topics of conversation were limited to domestic ones, particularly local gossip. In her early journals, Lister recorded many such visits she made to neighboring families to take tea with the ladies. She enjoyed parlaying their questions, which clearly indicated she was a frequent subject of gossip, into more positive accounts of her nontraditional activities. In *Emma*, Austen used taking tea to show how boring women's gossip could be and to demonstrate how effeminate Emma's father had become when having his old female neighbors to tea was the day's highlight.

TRAVEL AND AESTHETICS

Women of the leisured classes took tea in each others' homes while gentlemen attended clubs and businessmen frequented coffee shops. In the country, men of leisure could indulge themselves in sports such as riding horses or in **curricles** (the sports car of the day), or hunting pheasants and other game, while women were still confined to the home or garden except for group excursions. More extended rural entertainments for the leisure ranks included touring, either in short trips to established locations known for their **picturesque** views, or in extended trips to locations whose landscapes were known for their **beauty** or their **sublimity**. These trips within the British Isles were a domestic version of the Grand Tour, the several-month trip to the Continent that a young man of privilege would take with his tutor in order to complete his education. But whereas the Grand Tour was intended to cultivate the young aristocrat or gentleman, with stops in Paris, Rome, and perhaps a few other Italian cities known for their art and society, domestic tours were made by family members in order to develop an aesthetic sensibility for nature. Travel, unlike balls, theater, sports, or shopping, was the one entertainment meant to be educative and enlightening.

At the beginning of the Romantic period, British readers were introduced to the new aesthetic theory of the picturesque through the publication of William Gilpin's *Observations on the River Wye, and Several Parts of South Wales, etc. Relative Chiefly to Picturesque Beauty; made in the Summer of the Year 1770*, published in 1782. Although the concept of "pittoresco" was an innovation of the Italian Renaissance, it only arrived in Britain with Gilpin's handbook on how to view a landscape as if a framed painting. His tutorial showed travelers where to stand to take in the view properly and what to admire about it. Austen makes fun of the picturesque in several novels, most notably in *Northanger Abbey* when Henry and Eleanor Tilney teach the ignorant Catherine about the picturesque, and again in *Pride and Prejudice* when Elizabeth jokes that if she joined the others in their garden stroll, she should ruin their symmetry:

> "No, no; stay where you are. You are charmingly grouped, and appear to uncommon advantage. The picturesque would be spoilt by admitting a fourth. Good-bye."
>
> (*Pride and Prejudice* 80)

Paintings that demonstrated the picturesque would artfully balance symmetrical with asymmetrical forms so that a distorted tree might be in the foreground to the right, three rural figures or some cows might be in the distant middle ground, and majestic mountains might dominate the horizon. The symmetrical forms were associated with the beautiful, and the asymmetrical with the sublime, so that the picturesque created a domesticated, rationalized version of both. One took in the view as if it was a painting; the landscape was in this way tamed, associated with paintings made for the parlor wall.

If the picturesque taught one how to see properly, other entertainments – particularly those of large towns and especially London – were venues where one endeavored to be seen. Balls and theaters were particularly associated with this aspect of social life. To be invisible at a ball was to utterly fail at the task of being recognized as belonging to the elite group of people who count, whether as dance partners, elite ladies who come to view the others, or as discerning men. Whatever one's role, it was important to be seen, and to be seen being seen. This aspect of social life was even more elevated at the theater, where the play enacted on stage was never the main reason for coming; one needed to be seen and paid court to by others. For this reason, box seats were especially sought after since they made the sitter more visible, and theater managers began to capitalize on this by providing seating at the edge of stages so that more privileged male members of the audience could be positioned there. It afforded those theatergoers more visibility but also cunningly directed the audience's eyes toward the stage and the players. Theater managers resorted to such devices because audience members used the theater as meeting places, the men getting up mid-scene to visit a friend in a box, or making an assignation with an actress in the green room waiting to go onstage. Romantic period actors such as Mary Robinson and comic actors such as Dorothy Jordan, unlike the great tragedians Edward Keen and Sarah Siddons, became known for their beauty and liveliness rather than their art. Robinson and Jordan were unusual for another reason: onstage to act, offstage they both became royal mistresses, a spectacle of another caliber that made them the object of society columns and celebrities. Unlike balls, theaters were venues where celebrity and spectacle intermixed.

One can say then that one element of the period's cultural imagination is the spectacle or exhibition itself. This was an entertainment that brought the exotic home. Encountering the exotic, whether this meant other non-Western cultures, the ancient past, or non-native animals, was a way of experiencing the increasing reaches of global travelers without having to travel oneself. One exhibition, titled "The Esquimaux Indians" and arranged by Samuel Hadlock, a whaling captain, placed an Inuit couple from Baffin Island on display in their native dress. Oddly, and a seeming mismatch, it was held at the Egyptian Hall in Piccadilly, London, although it is the very contradiction of Indigenous and ancient cultures represented by the display and venue that exemplifies Regency taste.

The Egyptian Hall was an extraordinary spectacle hall commissioned by William Bullock as a museum for his large collection of curiosities, which included items from the South Seas brought back by Captain Cook. Completed in 1812 at the beginning of the Regency, and in true Regency style (which could be neoclassical or exotic with Egyptian, Chinese, or Arabic designs), it was built to look like an Ancient Egyptian temple. Because of the dramatic nature of its interior, it quickly became the ideal venue for exhibitions; a sense of what it must have been like to enter that space can be gained by a trip to Harrods today in Knightsbridge, London. That emporium was originally established in 1824 in Southwark as a draper's, mercer's, and a haberdasher's that sold fabric, expensive textiles, sewing notions, or men's wear. Harrods now has 330 departments in buildings occupying five acres, a far cry from its origins, but the connection to the Egyptian Hall can be found in the spectacular Egyptian staircase that reproduces at an exaggerated scale what an ancient Egyptian palace or large temple might have been like, complete with columns topped with Hathor heads (Hathor was Ra's consort, a sky goddess who represented feminine beauty), while in the clothing hall enormous lotus-topped columns and a giant gilded pharaoh's head dominate the scene. Such a grand scale and sumptuous design give an idea of what it must have been for displays at the original Egyptian Hall. The exotic seemed even more exotic, the distant past seemed even more historically different and strange. And yet, having living displays or grand-scale spectacles also made these cultures or pasts come alive. That paradox, as well as display, is typical of the Regency.

THE REGENCY: A PARADOX

As a discrete period within the Romantic period, the Regency presents its own paradox: it was both a time when radicals such as Percy Shelley despaired of seeing their revolutionary ideas transform society, and critical thinkers like Mary Shelley drew a dark picture of such possibilities ever taking place, as in her novel *The Last Man*. And yet at the same time consumerism, fashion, and the sheer social exuberance promoted by the Prince Regent's lifestyle and consumerist fantasies made everyday life for middle-class and elite families seemingly a whir of activity and pleasure. At the same time, some activities embodied the Regency's paradoxical nature, such as the **Reform Club**, established to support Chartism, a working-class movement often misreported in the newspapers and feared by middling and upper classes (Chase 4–6). The Reform Club was composed of elite and powerful men devoted to enlarging voting rights ("the franchise") to men not entitled to vote: the laboring classes (Fagan 12–13). However, doing good apparently requires being good to yourself: the Club built itself an enormous and quite beautiful meeting hall near the St. James Palace that still has active memberships. A gentleman's club, it provided spaces for meeting, dining, reading newspapers, and other quiet activities, and also congenial activities such as card playing and partying. Designed with elegant columns, halls, high ceilings, and different kinds of spaces, the huge Reform Club building is a testament to the Regency's high opinion of its own worth.

Paradoxically, the Regency was also a time when women writers were the most popular novelists, poets, and travel writers of the period despite the reduced chances of feminism gaining lost ground. **Circulating libraries** were already dominating the book market for those unable or unwilling to purchase every title; for a small annual subscription, one had access to hundreds of titles in the largest of these libraries. In smaller towns, the circulating library might be a few titles available at a general goods store, but even these were sure to have the most popular titles such as Ann Radcliffe's Gothics or travel writing. And travel writing was increasingly the province of women who were traveling to the Caribbean and the Middle East. Their eye for social life made women's travel writing more ethnographic (describing how people in other cultures experienced their daily lives) as opposed to men's travel writing, which tended to describe a city's or country's military preparedness, natural resources, trade, and economic health. Men's travel writing was encyclopedic; women's was personal. With more and more women making up the reading public, it is easy to see why women's writing might have become more and more popular, but in fact, women writers were popular with all kinds of readers.

The Regency was a particularly exhilarating time to be alive for the elite. In these social ranks, whether a landowner (aristocracy and gentry) or successful in trade or industry (upper-middling ranks), one had the leisure and wealth to partake in social activities such as invitation-only balls, routs, masquerades, concerts, plays and operas, exhibitions, touring, and gambling parties. All provided opportunities for social engagement beyond the confines of the family and were viewed as networking opportunities. Social events gained particular importance during the Regency as families with newer wealth, whether from industry and trade at home or in India, sought to marry their children into the landed ranks (old wealth and estates with greater social status). In a time when banks were not insured and vulnerable to bankruptcy, the stability of land made it a highly prized form of familial wealth and yet often the landed families benefited from marriages with the newly wealthy.

The exhilaration of the Regency, then, came from two directions. First, the increased rate of industrial production and global trade meant that the upper-middling ranks had more money, and this drove an increasing consumer appetite. Consumerism was stimulated by the need to imitate the aristocracy through increased acquisition of clothes – not only more clothes, but specialized for different activities, and livery for coachmen and footmen – all of which represented the family's wealth. Clothing allowances were important for the middling classes as well as those who owned a townhouse and a country house. Even without a large establishment, fine furniture and dishware, and the ability to throw elegant parties to attract those of higher rank were important to social respectability. Second, increased industrial productivity made the children of upper-middling families desirable to the upper classes whose finances required stabilizing. That need was often the result of poor estate management, loss of male farm laborers to the military, as well as to the aristocratic practice of patrilineal succession. This practice meant that only the eldest son, or in some cases the nearest male relative, could inherit the father's title and estate. Eldest sons of aristocratic families would come into at least part of their inheritance when they came of age, enabling them to gamble away large fortunes at cards and other forms of betting, a diversion from the boredom of not having a career due to their rank. The same began to be true for eldest sons in families striving to join the upper ranks. And for elite families, locating a wealthy middling-rank heiress for such a son meant that the kind of rigid caste divisions that characterized European society were not as significant an element in British family alliances. This was even more the case during the Regency when the wars with France had decreased the number of available young men, the wealth of the middling ranks was increasing faster, and an increasing sense of patriotism meant that looking for a marital partner should be done at home, not abroad. And so never were balls so important as during the Regency when leisure, wealth, and land came together to signal a rejuvenation of British blood and spirit. The worry over

French decadence and its effects on native British vigor that had characterized the anti-revolutionary rhetoric of the 1790s resulted in part in a Regency revitalization as a way to put "Merry Old England" above continental manners and education.

But the Regency paradox is that this renewed vigor translated as renewed excess for the elite and monied ranks alone. And this vigorous excess meant that what the empire and global trade brought home in terms of fabrics and foods (cotton and dyes from India, tea from India and China, coffee and opium from Turkey, cocoa and tobacco from the Americas) became a part of British culture. This had already been the case for the very wealthy, but now middling families could experience these and other kinds of consumption. One form of consuming other cultures that was newly available to non-elites was of design. "Oriental" architecture and interior design became popular, rivaling the earlier Gothic style: "Oriental" mainly meant Indian and Arabic, although Chinese-inspired styles and motifs were closely associated with the term (Morley 67, 338). Known as "**Chinoiserie**," Chinese design was already established by the late 1700s with influences ranging from the blue "willow" designs painted on imported porcelain to lacquer furniture and silk fabrics for those wealthy enough to afford them. These were adapted for Chinese hand-painted wallpaper, and "Chinese"-style decorative items, tableware, and furniture. Now that such objects and designs were more available for consumers, styles began to overlap so that Gothic, Chinoiserie, and Oriental designs could designate particular rooms not only in grand homes but even in more modest houses such as Sir John Soane's house by Lincoln's Inn Fields in London.

A good example of mixed styles in a grand house is the Prince Regent's summer pavilion at Brighton. The Prince of Wales had considered himself to be the "first gentleman of Europe" well before becoming Regent. In fact, he began the construction of the **Royal Pavilion** in 1787 when his two residences in London were overfilled with his collections of art and antiquities. The pavilion was originally a neoclassical rotunda with three large rooms; it was extensively enlarged in 1815 at the height of the Regency to indulge the Prince's taste for excitement and excess. With the 1815 remodeling, the pavilion looks on the outside like a miniature palace airlifted from India. It was built in the Indo-Saracenic or **Mughal style** then dominant in India, which mixed native architectural elements with the minarets and domes of the conquering Islamic culture, while on the inside the décor was first in the Chinoiserie style, and later mixed with the Oriental style (Loske 123).

Here the Regent could privately entertain his lifelong mistress Maria Fitzherbert and indulge in his passion for gambling without the court's knowledge. More importantly, he could hold extravagant multi-day parties where guests could partake of multiple-course banquets served up by the Regent's large cook staff in a kitchen truly fit for a king. The Regent took particular pains with the design of this kitchen, since it needed to be able to produce feasts on a magnificent scale, and the Great Kitchen was intended from the start to house a French chef. The Regent's clerk controller was sent to Paris to secure Antonin Carême for the position: Carême was chef to Napoleon and other great figures of the era and known as the first celebrity chef. The 1817 menu from a banquet in honor of Archduke Nicholas of Russia's visit lists "eight soups, eight *releves de Poisson*, fifteen *Assiettes Volantes a Servir Apres les Poissons*, eight *grosses pieces*, forty *entrees*, eight *pieces montees*, eight roasts and thirty-two *entremets*," and "twelve *Assiettes Volantes*" for dessert (Kelly, *Cooking* 134–40). As Ian Kelly points out, this astounding menu, which was for the last of three banquets on consecutive nights given for the Russian entourage, was meant as a spectacle and statement of excess rather than to be eaten, since "no one—not even the gluttonous Prince Regent—could have sampled more than a fraction of the whole" (Kelly, 141). The British and Russian monarchies celebrated their political alliance through this gastronomic theater. It was over the top even for the Regency, however, and the Prince was so unpopular by 1817 for his excessive spending that stones were thrown on his way to the State Opening of Parliament (Kelly 127).

The pavilion's architectural elements of the minarets and domes added in 1815 and the alteration of the interior design from Chinoiserie to Oriental signaled a cultural turn toward a fantasy version of the Middle East and South Asia that is imaginatively captured in William Beckford's novel *Vathek*, discussed in Chapter four. Both the elements of Vathek's palace of the senses and of Beckford's own inherited estate, which he staged as a vast Oriental interior for his coming-of-age birthday party, can be seen played out in smaller scale in the Brighton pavilion. However, the Regent's London residence, Carleton House, had a Gothic conservatory adjoining the dining room so that *Vathek's* sensual aesthetic could be felt there as well (Kelly, *Cooking* 126). At Brighton, the music room and banquet hall in particular recall scenes from the novel where Vathek, grandson of the great ruler Haroun Al Raschid, was a self-indulgent libertine as unlike his predecessors as possible – much like the Prince Regent. There were five wings to Vathek's magnificent palace, "which he destined for the particular gratification of each of his senses." The first and most important was the "Eternal, or Unsatiating Banquet" in which "were tables continually covered with the most exquisite dainties, which were supplied both by night and by day according to their constant consumption; whilst the most delicious wines, and the choicest cordials, flowed forth from a hundred fountains, that were never exhausted" (Beckford 46). Although the Prince Regent did not aspire to this level of splendor, he did aim to have the finest table in Britain. His kitchens had the most advanced technology, capable of producing up to 70 dishes for a banquet, with an innovative steam table to keep foods warm until served. In addition to the central kitchen, there were auxiliary kitchens including five pastry and confectionary ones (Kelly, *Cooking* 123).

The second wing of Vathek's palace "was styled 'The Temple of Melody, or the Nectar of the Soul.' It was inhabited by the most skillful musicians and admired poets of the time, who not only displayed their talents within, but dispersing in bands without, caused every surrounding scene to reverberate their songs, which were continually varied in the most delightful succession" (Beckford 46). While the Regent's music room was quite small in comparison, it was centrally located so that the musicians playing during large parties could be heard throughout the main sections of the pavilion. These two examples, the pavilion's banquet hall and music room, reveal how Orientalism was associated not just with interior décor but with sensory indulgence. Because Beckford's novel spends so much of its plot on such indulgence and its sexualized sensations – and especially on excess, whether foods and wines, incense and perfumed vapors, or delightful music – its particular version of Orientalism was very appealing to a period in which the British became more and more confident of their ability to defeat French imperialism, consumerism was constantly on the rise, manufacturing innovations were reaching new high points, and global trade was bringing exotic goods to exhibitions and to the shops.

CELEBRITIES

The celebrity is one whose individualism is heightened to the level of spectacle: the individual not as a romantic soul but as a spirit of the times. Although there were a large number of celebrated persons during the Romantic period in Britain, the term "celebrity" did not come into usage in the sense we now give it until the Regency, and arguably if Antonin Carême was the first celebrity chef, Lord Byron was the first international celebrity, eventually to become after his death the first global celebrity (see Mole and Tuite). But before them there were a number of notables who must be distinguished from members of the court and elite society; the doings of the latter regularly made the gossip columns or were detailed in periodicals such as the fashion magazine *La Belle Assemblée or, Bell's Court and Fashionable Magazine Addressed Particularly to the Ladies* and more general *Lady's Monthly Museum; or Entertaining Companion for the Fair Sex, Appropriated Solely to Their Use and Amusement*. Most of those who were in the public's eye who were not of the aristocracy or members of the court were upper-middle or middle rank intellectuals and artists, or those who claimed the public's interest by developing close ties with royalty or the aristocracy. These included Beau Brummell, Mary Robinson, Banastre Tarleton, and Charlotte Smith. The Prince Regent himself, known as "Prinny" in elite circles, was really in this group in that his reputation for idiosyncrasy and audacious behavior exceeded what was expected or normally tolerated in royals. But only Byron, and perhaps Robinson and Brummell, could be said to be celebrities in that their reputations and behavior made them objects of public interest beyond the boundaries of normally notable figures. There are others, however, who enjoyed a more quiet celebrity and who should be mentioned.

The Ladies of Llangollen were Irish noblewomen, Eleanor Butler and Sarah Ponsonby, who escaped parental control to live together in seclusion in Wales as "romantic friends." This term was used to indicate an intense friendship between two women that was considered affectionate but not sexual; it was used by lesbians to conceal what was otherwise illicit sexuality, termed "Sapphism" – a word used to excoriate women in the public eye such as Marie Antoinette and her court by accusing them of unmentionable behavior without grounds. "Romantic friends," also without grounds, were assumed to be in a platonic, though affectionate, relationship as an acceptable way for unmarried women to support themselves financially. The Ladies of Llangollen, however, became known for their high level of intellectuality, and began receiving visitors that eventually included the poet Anna Seward, Wordsworth, Coleridge, the young Percy Shelley and Lord Byron, Sir Walter Scott, the influential pottery entrepreneur Josiah Wedgwood, Anne Lister, and the Duke of Wellington. Each visitor felt that to have met the ladies was to have had an important experience. The young Byron left them a volume of his poetry, hoping for their approval.

Beau Brummell represents the other extreme; he was hardly quiet and manufactured his own celebrity quite carefully. An intimate of the Prince Regent and Mrs. Fitzherbert, George Bryan Brummell had risen to such social heights through bravado and performance. Although his parents were from the middle ranks of society, they both worked in government positions, and Brummell was raised to have high expectations. In 1794, he was able to purchase a lowly commission in the Prince's Tenth Royal Hussars, and this gained him the Prince's notice; from there, he fashioned himself into a notable dandy and the arbiter of taste for men's fashion. A dandy is a man who puts fashion above all, and Brummell styled the quintessential dress for dandies: subtle colors, tight-fitting clothes, highly polished boots, and an enormous stock (neckcloth) tied elaborately inside a stiffly starched shirt collar. More than that, Brummell exemplified the dandy of wit and nonchalant elegance; he played the courtier but as one that any somewhat privileged young man could emulate. He also lived like a courtier, but one to whom others paid court. People visited to see if they could catch him at his famously long dressing routine to find out his fashion secrets; less secret were his fastidious cleanliness in an age where being clean was not yet prized. But he is remembered as much for his witty sayings and repartee as for his dress. His downfall was both his gambling and witticisms that gambled on cutting remarks being valued above the receiver's pride; he lost on both counts, famously cutting the Regent who immediately dropped him.

Mary Robinson was more like Brummell than the Llangollen pair. She was famous first as an actress who, on capturing the eye of the young Prince of Wales, became a royal mistress, although only for a year. Now more continually in the public eye, she took advantage of her new role with extravagant gowns and hats, multiple carriages, and jewelry provided by the Prince. She was said to be the most beautiful woman in England, and when she visited Versailles to meet Marie Antoinette herself in the years before the French Revolution, the queen called her "La belle Anglaise," a term of praise that accompanied her throughout her life. Even after losing the favors of the Prince, Robinson retained her celebrity status, which was responsible in part for the sales of her books. She was known for her poetry as "the English Sappho" (**Sappho** here indicates a woman poet; being "Sapphic" referred to lesbianism), and for her acting as "Perdita," the Shakespearean role for which she became famous because that was the role for which the Prince fell in love with her as he watched her perform it on stage. Her first book of poems was written while staying with her husband in debtor's prison for his gambling debts; she then became an actress, a job that, like writing, allowed her to support her infant daughter and remain independent of her irresponsible spouse. However, she was tutored in acting by the great David Garrick, so that she was given central roles; she had similarly high expectations for her poetry and novels, and the public responded by making her one of the best-selling writers of her day. Scholars argue that she ranks among the preeminent women celebrities of the modern era (Fay 192–3).

But Lord Byron was inarguably *the* celebrity of his day from 1812, with the publication of *Childe Harold* Cantos I and II, to his death in 1824. More than the other celebrities, his was flavored with notoriety, which changed the way celebrity was understood thereafter (Tuite 4). By the time Anne Lister was reading and discussing literature with friends in the 1830s, Byron's works and name were invoked to express one's sensibility, taste, and literary education, as well as a way to determine like-minded persons. Byron had become a barometer of literary taste and would remain so through the Victorian period that followed. As early as Austen's *Persuasion*, published posthumously in 1817, Byron indicates one's refined taste for both Anne Elliot's friend Lady Russell and for one of her love interests, Captain Benwick. Tellingly for Austen's point of view, Anne finds Byron too inducive of melancholy and suggests a diet of moral prose for Benwick instead, who is recovering from a great loss. Loss of a loved one is a staple of Byron's works, from earlier works like "Epistle to Augusta" to his Turkish Tales, each of which features an adventurer who loses or has lost his beloved and now attempts to make amends for that loss, to *Manfred*, in which the protagonist agonizes over the loss of his beloved sister. Each of these lost loved ones is surrounded by secrecy or are objects of forbidden love in some way, such as Leila in *The Giaour* (1813), who is the youngest wife in Hassan's harem and is executed for her elopement with the Venetian Giaour. In return for her death, he wrecks carnage on Hassan and his court. As he confesses at the end of his life,

> "And she was lost—and yet I breathed
> But not the breath of human life—
> A serpent round my heart was wreathed,
> And stung my every thought to strife."
>
> *(192–5)*

This confession of a great loss combined with vengeance, both of which were outside the bounds of morality and yet of which are painted with a heroic brush (Leila is married against her will, Hassan is a brutal husband and ruler), are key elements of the "**Byronic hero**." A combination of outlaw and chivalrous knight, the Byronic hero appeals to lovers of medieval romance, pirate stories, and star-crossed or forbidden love. Byron had created the perfect model for his protagonists: comfortable in a Gothic,

Ottoman, historical, or present-day setting, this character represents both the dark and the courageous aspects of conflicted heroism. He is a loner or in exile; his passionate interiority is incompatible with normal society; his talents are wasted for lack of compatible environment or companions; and he harbors a dark secret – all of these combine to make an irresistible protagonist.

The Byronic hero was Byron's own invention modeled on his own personality, although it was very much one he cultivated and promoted, just as Beau Brummell developed his public persona as the preeminent dandy. Role playing such as Brummell and Byron engaged in is instrumental to creating a cult of personality, and for both men the public character came to supplant the private one until each was beholden to the public face they had created. By the time of Byron's death in Greece, where he was aiding the Greek resistance to Ottoman rule, he had gained a truly heroic stature. When his embalmed body was returned to London, huge crowds attended the two-day viewing of his coffin before he was buried in the family vault near his ancestral estate Newstead Abbey in Nottinghamshire. He remains a national hero in Greece, and his influence was felt throughout Continental culture and literature where in many nations he is still ranked among the greatest poets.

REGENCY COROLLARIES

Whereas the Regency is a period particular to Britain, other romanticisms such as German and Italian romanticism had their own period of vibrant activity. And like the Regency, they were dominated by celebrities like Byron, or by literary figures whose influence was felt internationally as Byron's was. For Germany, the corollary to Britain's Regency was that of German Idealism when philosophical and artistic circles arose following Immanuel Kant's intellectual interventions. Although the larger German romantic movement, called "Storm und Drang" and dominated by Johann Wolfgang von Goethe and his circle, arose in protest against the Enlightenment's elevation of reason over intuition and imagination, German Idealism centered on theorizing a subjective account of reality as perceived through an individual's sensibility. The circle working in this line that was most like the Regency in its characteristic paradoxes included Friedrich and August

Schlegel, Caroline Schlegel, Novalis, and Friedrich Wilhelm Joseph Schelling (whose father was an Orientalist professor). Schelling was also friends with Hölderlin, Hegel, and Goethe, but it was the earlier circle of the Schlegels that produced the most vibrant mix of intellectual and artistic thought. It was also the circle most influenced by women's genius, including Dorothea Veit, daughter of Moses Mendelssohn. Led by the Schlegels, the group produced the radical journal *The Athenaeum*, which through a mix of aphorisms, fragments, and essays, articulated the group's vision of subjective idealism (Engel 77–81). This was also the position most like the mix of radical and conservative thought in the work of Percy and Mary Shelley; each group exemplifies the contradictions of romanticism generally, which only intensified in the latter part of the era.

Other corollaries include American Transcendentalism led by Bronson Alcott, Louisa May Alcott's father, and featured the works of Henry David Thoreau and Ralph Waldo Emerson, both of whom combined philosophical thought with individual sensibility; the Polish flourishing of romanticism in expatriate circles in the early 1830s where nationalism and mysticism interwove; and the Italian romantic movement centered on Alessandro Manzoni, whose mix of philosophy and liberal politics made him the voice of the new Italian literature and the "living" Italian language of a unified people. In South American romanticism, the period most analogous to the Regency is the third period, which turned the deep emotionality of the earlier romantics toward political topics, especially abolition. The Brazilian poet and politician Pedro Luís Pereira de Sousa is particularly important for this movement.

All of these romanticisms chart in similar ways how the political radicalization of the individual then opened up one's thought, imagination, and appetite to the wider world and all it had to offer. This, in fact, is the legacy of romanticism.

SUMMARY

The Regency encapsulates the Romantic era, intensifying some key elements such as love of spectacle, consumerism, the individual (intensified into celebrity), and globalism (condensed into travel).

- Balls became especially important during the Regency, since the wars had diminished the number of eligible men and competition in the marriage market was increased.
- Social life for the middling and wealthy classes also revolved around visiting spa towns, attending exhibitions, and taking tea.
- Even working-class political agitation (the Chartist movement) created an opportunity for wealthy men to club by creating the Reform Club.
- Travel created a way to experience the world firsthand, beyond imported goods and imitative designs such as Chinoiserie and Orientalism. Even travel to other parts of Britain created a new way of seeing, translated by aesthetic theory – especially that of the picturesque.
- The Regency was essentially paradoxical in its combination of radical and conservative sympathies.

FURTHER READING

Louis Fagan's chatty 1897 history *The Reform Club* includes a survey of the rise of the London club culture and of the rise of the St. James and Pall Mall area (digitized on Archive.org). Ian Kelly's *Cooking for Kings*, a biography of the first celebrity chef, provides incredible details about Brighton Pavilion at the height of its excesses. *The Epicure's Almanack*, Ralph Rylance's 1815 guide to Regency London eateries, gives a good sense of what public life was like. Venetia Murray's *An Elegant Madness* covers domestic as well as public aspects of Regency life.

WEBSITES

Atelier Nostalgia: Historical Accuracy—Regency https://ateliernostalgia.wordpress.com/2016/05/23/historical-accuracy-regency/.

Jane Austen Society. https://janeaustensociety.org.uk/.

JASNA. https://jasna.org/.

Maggie May Clothing. https://maggiemayfashions.com/calicoball/fashionhistory/the-late-georgian-empire-regency-era-1790-1820/.

The Regency Townhouse. https://www.rth.org.uk/regency-period.

V&A: Thomas Hope and the Regency Style. https://www.vam.ac.uk/articles/thomas-hope-and-the-regency-style?srsltid=AfmBOoojROQ8_IVqYelpiChMGMWd_ArqtZC5wBuPgv7OXkqw0Aju2e-K.

WORKS CITED

Anon. *Regency Etiquette: Mirror of Graces [Mirror of Graces, or the English Lady's Costume]*. Mendocino: R. L. Shep, 1997.

Austen, Jane. *Pride and Prejudice*. Edited by Robert P. Irvine. 2nd ed. Peterborough: Broadview, 2020.

Beckford, William. *Vathek*. Edited by Kenneth Graham. Peterborough: Broadview, 2001.

Byron, George Gordon. *The Giaour*. London: John Murray, 1813.

Chase, Malcolm. *Chartism: A New History*. Manchester: Manchester University Press, 2007.

Engel, Manfred. "The Aesthetics of German Idealism and Its Reception in European Romanticism." In *Nonfictional Romantic Prose: Expanding Borders*, edited by Steven Sondrup, Virgil Nemoianu, and Gerald Gillespie, 69–95. Amsterdam: John Benjamins, 2004.

Fagan, Louis. *The Reform Club: Its Founders and Architect*. London: Bernard Quaritch, 1897.

Fay, Elizabeth. *Fashioning Faces: The Portraitive Mode in British Romanticism*. Durham: University Press of New England, 2010.

Forsyth, Michael. *Pevsner Architectural Guides: Bath*. New Haven: Yale University Press, 2004.

Kelly, Ian. *Beau Brummell: The Ultimate Dandy*. London: Hodder & Stoughton, 2005.

Kelly, Ian. *Cooking for Kings: The Life of Antonin Carême, the First Celebrity Chef*. London: Walker Books, 2005.

Kowaleski-Wallace, Elizabeth. *Consuming Subjects: Women, Shopping, and Business in the Eighteenth Century*. New York: Columbia University Press, 1996.

Loske, Alexandra. *The Royal Pavilion, Brighton: A Regency Palace of Colour and Sensation*. New Haven: Yale University Press, 2025.

Lynch, Deirdre. *The Economy of Character: Novels, Market Culture, and the Business of Inner Meaning*. Chicago: University of Chicago Press, 1998.

Mole, Tom. *Romanticism and Celebrity Culture, 1750–1850*. Cambridge: Cambridge University Press, 2009.

Morley, John. *Regency Design 1790–1840*. New York: Harry N. Abrams, 1993.

Murray, Venetia. *An Elegant Madness: High Society in Regency England*. London: Penguin, 2000.

Rylance, Ralph. *The Epicure's Almanack: Eating and Drinking in Regency London*. Edited by Janet Ing Freeman. London: The British Library, 2012.

Tuite, Clara. *Lord Byron and Scandalous Celebrity*. Cambridge: Cambridge University Press, 2014.

GLOSSARY

Abolition: political activism to end the slave trade. Although abolition occurred periodically throughout history, romanticism parallels the first modern attempts to abolish human trafficking. In Britain, The Slave Trade Act 1807 was passed by the British Parliament after activists began agitating in the early 1780s.

Aesthetics: a philosophically based system of judging natural and artistic beauty. It was divided into concepts of the sublime, the beautiful, and the picturesque. Edmund Burke proposed a systematic examination of the concepts, which Immanuel Kant then refined in his *Critique of Judgment.*

Alchemy: the medieval form of natural philosophy, a pseudoscientific endeavor. The greatest medieval alchemists prepared the ground for modern science.

American romanticism: embraced the themes of individualism, nature, and affective, intuitive understanding but emerged several decades later than European romanticisms and so revolution was less important than a national identity.

Ancien régime: used by French revolutionists for traditional rule by monarchy and aristocracy which they wanted to overthrow. Adapted by the British who saw their parliamentary system as a version of democratic rule.

Anti-Jacobin (see Jacobin): refers to reactionary writers and groups who attacked radical public figures favoring the French revolutionaries.

Beautiful: aesthetic category; experiences in nature and art that invoke harmony and pleasure.

Black romanticism: literary and cultural movement originating in Caribbean colonies; applies romantic themes of individualism and imagination to Black experience.

Bluestocking: a woman who attempted to be educated in the same subjects as men.

Botanical Society of Lichfield: founded by Erasmus Darwin in 1787, it was a society of three men established to translate and publish Linnaeus's sexual classification system for plants.
This translation was published by the Botanical Society at Lichfield in 1787.

Brighton Pavilion: *see* Royal Pavilion

British Museum: founded in 1757 with the collections of naturalist Sir Hans Sloane, it was developed as a "universal museum" to include historical and cultural artworks and an extensive library; it is the first national museum opened to the public in the world.

Brown romanticism: denotes literature by Indian writers who used romantic tropes and aesthetics; it particularly refers to Indian English poetry.

Buck: a man of leisure who put bloodsports above all, and who could engage in ungentlemanly violence when drunk.

Byronic hero: persona created by Byron based on his own aloofness and self-alienation.

Catholic Emancipation: movement to remove restrictions in Britain and Ireland that disallowed Catholics from attending Oxford and Cambridge, holding public office, voting, and practicing Catholicism openly.

Chartism: British working-class movement for political reform, concentrated in areas dependent on one industry (e.g., pottery) that lasted from 1838 to 1857.

Chhayavad: romantic poetry written in Hindi.

Chinoiserie: interior design, furniture, and ceramics that reflect Asian influence and aesthetics.

Circulating libraries: subscription libraries, often located in a general shop; members could borrow books too expensive to buy; the membership fee, however, was still above what lower-class readers could afford.

Classical period (French): period covering the French Revolution and the Napoleonic aftermath, previous to the rise of French romanticism.

Closet drama: a drama in verse not intended to be staged. These were written in imitation of ancient Greek dramas, which were read in the period as poems rather than produced for the stage. A good example is Percy Shelley's *Prometheus Unbound*.

Curricle: a fashionable lightweight vehicle with two large wheels drawn by two horses and driven by the owner; it was the equivalent of a sports car.

Dandy: man of leisure who emphasized his sartorial appearance, often imitating Beau Brummell's dress.

Deism: rational theology associated with the Enlightenment.

Demi Monde: the world of courtesans at the edges of respectable society.

Dissenters: in England and Wales, a religious sect dissenting from the Anglican Church; like Catholics, Dissenters could not attend Oxford or Cambridge, or hold public office.

Doubled heroine: novelistic device in which two heroines of contrasting character together represent an ideal femininity.

East India Company: 1600–1874; formed to trade in the East Indies, it expanded to trade with the Far East and control much of India.

Emancipation Act (The Slavery Abolition Act 1833): British parliamentary act to purchase the freedom of all slaves in British territories, the end goal of abolition.

Enlightenment: the 18th-century movement in Europe and Britain that placed reason and empiricism above tradition and superstition, and promoted individual rights and religious tolerance.

Estates General: advisory body to the French monarch composed of three estates: clergy, nobility, and commoners.

Female Friendship: term for a female couple, considered nonsexual even when cohabiting.

Female Husband: term for a married transman.

Free Love: radical sexual relationship intended to disrupt the institution of marriage in which husbands "possess" wives.

Georgian architecture: the dominant style from 1714 to 1830, it emphasized symmetry and proportion, considered the major characteristics of Ancient Greek and Roman architecture.

German Idealism: philosophical movement emerging from Immanuel Kant's work influenced by romanticism and revolutionary politics.

German romanticism: emerged earliest, in the 1770s; the phase when art and intellectualism centered in Jena produced innovative thought; major figures include Goethe, Heine, and Hoffmann.

Gothic craze: the period during which Gothic novels, plays, and poetry were all the rage in Britain; cresting in the 1790s, it reflected the similar horror fascination as news about the French Revolution aroused.

Grecian style: interior design, furniture, and household goods reflecting Neoclassical values, particularly as influenced by antiquarian research such as James Stuart and Nicolas Revett's multi-volume *Antiquities of Athens* (1762), and by Sir William Hamilton's publication of his collection, *Collection of Etruscan, Greek, and Roman Antiquities* (1766–67).

Greek love: code term used for illegal homosexual acts, particularly with younger men or boys. The term derived from the correspondence of boys' schools and the study of Greek authors who wrote about same-sex love.

Haitian Revolution: the successful overthrow of French colonial rule in Saint-Domingue, now Haiti. Its charismatic leader was Toussaint Louverture, who gained heroic stature in the romantic pantheon due to both his achievement and his martyrdom by the French.

Horror gothics: gothic literature emphasizing supernatural and demonic elements, with violent plots usually including incest, torture, and murder.

Individual: the concept of a subject with free will, imagination, and taste, and the capacity to pursue their ambitions.

Imagination: the romantic concept of artistic imagination; a mental faculty of creativity, inspiration, and daring mental experiments.

Italian romanticism: combined emphasis on individualism, emotionalism, nature, and imagination with cultural heritage but also the dream of a united polity.

Jacobin (see Anti-Jacobin): politicians, intellectuals, and artists who argued in favor of the French Revolution. Mary Wollstonecraft wrote *Vindication of the Rights of Man* (1790) as part of this effort, for instance.

London Corresponding Society: a network of small debate clubs with working-class members with the purpose of agitating for parliamentary reform following French democratic achievements.

Lunar Society of Birmingham: informal club of intellectual and scientific men in the midlands meeting between 1765–1813.

Macartney Embassy: the first British diplomatic mission to China in 1793. In addition to the trade and policy goals of the mission, members carried out scientific and cultural studies.

Mansfield Decision: the 1772 decision in which Lord Mansfield settled the case of Somerset v. Stewart declaring any enslaved person on English soil could not be forcibly deported; thus escaping individuals sought England for safety.

Medievalism: revival of medieval architectural and design styles beginning in the last half of the 18th century.

Mesmerism: named after Franz Mesmer, who developed his theory of an energy transference between bodies into "animal magnetism," which he later termed "mesmerism," now hypnosis.

Mughal style: the architectural and design style developed during the Mughal Empire and encountered by Europeans traveling or working in India; it is characterized by minarets, onion domes, massive interior spaces, and intricate patterns in the décor.

Nabob: an Anglo-Indian term for Britons who became wealthy in 18th-century India, largely through the East India Company.

Napoleonic aftermath: refers to the restoration of monarchies and revised geopolitical boundaries after Napoleon's wars ended, as well as to the economic depression and food shortages experienced after his campaigns had devastated large sections of Europe.

Napoleonic Empire: established by Napoleon, who ruled as emperor from 1804 to 1815; a period of French dominance and political reform, followed by a return to monarchism after his death.

Natural history: emphasizes observation over experimentation, focusing on organisms in their natural environment.

Natural philosophy: a branch of philosophy, it was the study of nature and the physical universe; it was replaced by the modern sciences during the 18th and 19th centuries.

Nature poets: poets who used natural vistas or entities to explore romantic themes of the individual, the spiritual and transcendence, beauty, solitude, and alienation. They saw nature as a source of beauty, the sublime, and a living entity or force. In Britain specifically, it is used in reference to Wordsworth, Coleridge, and poets influenced by them.

Obi, Obeah: refers to West Indian religions of mixed African origins, with Christian and Indigenous influences, practiced by enslaved peoples and involving magic rituals and healing potions.

Orientalism: aesthetic term for a style of architecture, design, literature, and art that references Middle Eastern culture through a non-historical and prejudicial, imperial lens.

Picturesque: aesthetic term for landscapes that contain specific elements that combine symmetry, asymmetry, foreground and background with middleground, and can be viewed as if framed for a painting. Picturesque theory was developed by William Gilpin (1724–1804), whose books showed how to locate particular landscapes and view them properly.

Pleasure gardens: principally Vauxhall and Ranelagh, these were parks that offered Londoners evening concerts and other public entertainments; by the last half of the Romantic period they were more used as places of assignation.

Pneumatic chemistry: the study of gases and their chemical properties.

Private sphere: the private sphere was the proper one for middle and upper-class women because it was confined to domestic and interior spaces: the home, shops, carriages. Women of these classes were expected to confine themselves to conversation, embroidery and sewing, music or drawing, shopping for cloth, small goods or books, attending church on Sundays, and attending balls or plays when the chance arose.

Public sphere: the public sphere was defined as belonging to men of the middle and upper classes: it was where political debates, business, and intellectual discussions could take place.

Quest romance: a medieval genre of metrical verse concerning a knight dedicated to a quest either given to him or self-conceived; often used to explore romantic themes.

Reason: Enlightenment concept in which superstition could be eliminated through the elevation of rational thought at all times.

Red romanticism: refers to literature produced through contact with Native Americans or by writers of Anglo-Indigenous parentage.

Reform Act of 1832: expanded the vote to male small landowners, shopkeepers, and those paying enough rent.

Reform Club: a private gentlemen's club founded in 1836 by Whigs and Radicals to promote liberal political goals that the Reform Act embodied.

Regency: the period from 1811–1820 during which the Prince of Wales was nominally in charge, although Parliament actually governed.

Reign of Terror: period headed by Maximilien Robespierre, 1793–94, during which public executions and massacres took place.

Rights of Man: the concept of natural rights of the citizen, as opposed to absolute monarchy wherein the king defines individual liberty.

Rise of the novel: the emergence of the novel in the 18th century as a dominant literary form displaying realism, convoluted plots, and later protagonists capable of growth.

Romantic child: reconceives the child as attuned to nature and the divine, which it loses with socialization though trace memories can remain.

Royal Asiatic Society of Bengal: founded by Sir William Jones in 1784 to further research into India's history, culture, and languages for the benefit of the East India Company. Now the Asiatic Society, in Kolkata.

Royal Institution of Great Britain: founded in 1799 for scientific research, including mechanical innovation, and public education in the sciences. Its royal charter was granted in 1800.

Royal Pavilion (Brighton Pavilion): redesigned in the Mughal style, this was the Prince Regent's favorite venue for grand entertainments and huge feasts.

Royal Society: a learned society devoted to promoting scientific learning founded in 1660.

Sappho: Ancient Greek poet of Lesbos; it was a term of approbation for a woman poet of note such as Mary Robinson, not to be confused with "Sapphic," referring to lesbian sexual activity.

Slavers: term commonly used in the period for those engaged in capturing or gathering individuals for selling to others; it was also the term for ships used to transport captured Africans.

Socinianism: a Protestant school of thought that rejects the Trinity, the divinity of Christ, original sin, and the doctrine of salvation.

Spa town: resort town built around a natural spring whose mineral water was supposed to promote healing. Spa towns had venues for public entertainments such as balls, concerts, and theater.

Soul sleep: doctrine that the soul is dormant after death, awaiting rebirth. Romanticism amplified soul sleep to include the transcendence of mind-spirit associated with experiencing the sublime, and to suggest the possibility of communication with souls of the dead.

Sublime: aesthetic category for transcendent experiences of awe or terror induced by nature or art.

Terror gothics: gothic literature emphasizing the force of reason against superstition and expressing values of the middling classes.

Tory, Toryism: conservative party in British politics that supported the traditional social order under monarchy and opposed reform.

Transatlantic romanticism: merges romanticisms of colonial powers in the Atlantic.

Transcendentalism: aspect of early American romanticism opposing the individual's inherent goodness to society's corrupt influence; extends the "romantic child" concept to adulthood.

Travel writing: non-fiction writing by amateurs and explorers that provided readers with a vicarious travel experience. It often included descriptions of a country's military and economic status, cultural attributes and practices, local clothing and entertainments, and other details of foreign life. It was one of the most popular literary genres of the period.

Vitalism: theorizes that a vital principle is required to animate chemicals, creating living entities.

War with France: Britain's response to France's declaration of war in 1793 after the execution of Louis XVI.

Whig, Whiggism: liberal party in British politics advocating parliamentary restraint on the monarchy and oriented toward reform.

World geography: attempts to explore, map, and verify facts concerning all parts of the globe.

"Year without a summer": refers to 1816, when the volcanic eruption of Mount Tambora the previous year caused disastrous climate changes that caused record cold temperatures and adversely affected harvests.

ROMANTIC TIMELINE

Date	*Historical Events*	*Literature and Science*
1765		Percy, *Reliques of Ancient English Poetry*
1765		Walpole, *Castle of Otranto*
1767	First railroads built by Wilkinson	
1770	W. Wordsworth, Hegel, Beethoven born	
1771	D. Wordsworth born	
1772	Coleridge born; Hastings appointed governor of Bengal	
1772	The Mansfield Decision	
1775	Austen born	
1776	Mary Robinson debuts at Drury Lane as Juliet	
1780	Gordon Riots in London against Catholic Rights	Berthollet and Lavoisier isolate carbon, oxygen, and hydrogen
1783		Montgolfier makes first balloon ascent in France
1784	Pitt's India Act puts East India Company under royal authority; The Asiatic Society of Bengal founded	C. Smith, *Elegiac Sonnets, and Other Poems*; Cook, *Voyage to the Pacific Ocean in 1776–80*

Date	*Historical Events*	*Literature and Science*
1785	Sunday School Society founded to educate poor children	Jones, "A Hymn to Na'ra'yena"
1786	Boydell's Shakespeare Gallery opens, exhibiting scenes from recent Shakespeare productions	Beckford, *Vathek*; Clarkson, *An Essay on the Slavery and Commerce of the Human Species*; Mozart, *The Marriage of Figaro*
1787	Committee for the Abolition of the Slave Trade founded; Pitt the Younger and Wilberforce attempt to initiate an Anglo-French suspension of the slave trade	
1788	King George III's mental illness occasions the Regency Crisis (Burke and Charles Fox attack Pitt's ministry of attempting to obtain full regal powers for the Prince of Wales); trial of Warren Hastings for corruption in governing India; Estates General summoned by Louis XVI; Byron born	Clarkson, *Impolicy of the Slave Trade*; More, *Slavery: A Poem*; Yearsley, *A Poem on the Inhumanity of the Slave-Trade*
1789	Fall of the Bastille; *Declaration of the Rights of Man*; Wilberforce introduces resolutions on the slave trade in Parliament; Price gives his sermon, *Discourse on the Love of Our Country* to the London Revolution Society	Blake *Songs of Innocence,* begins *The Book of Thel* (1789–90); Equiano, *The Interesting Narrative of the Life of Olaudah Equiano*; Darwin, *Loves of the Plants* and *The Botanic Garden*; Lavoisier, *Elements of Chemistry*; Galvani's experiments on muscle contractions

Date	*Historical Events*	*Literature and Science*
1790	Jacobins gain power under Robespierre; French royal family captured attempting to flee; Washington delivers the first State of the Union address	Wollstonecraft, *Vindication of the Rights of Men*; Blake, *The Marriage of Heaven and Hell*; Williams, *Letters Written in France in the Summer of 1790*; Radcliffe, *The Sicilian Romance*; Kant, *Critique of Pure Reason*
1791	Haitian Revolution begins; Legislative Assembly convenes in Paris; Anti-Jacobin mob burns Priestley's house and laboratory	Paine, *The Rights of Man*, pt. 1; Radcliffe, *Romance of the Forest*; Barbauld, "Epistle To William Wilberforce"; Galvani posits "animal electricity"
1792	Abolition of the French monarchy; trial of Louis XVI	Wollstonecraft, *Vindication of the Rights of Woman*; Paine, *The Rights of Man*, pt. 2
1793	Execution of Louis XVI; France declares war on Britain, Holland and Spain; Reign of Terror; execution of Marie Antoinette	Godwin, *Enquiry Concerning Political Justice*; C. Smith, *The Emigrants*; Blake, *Songs of Experience, Visions of the Daughters of Albion*
1794	Robespierre executed; treason trials begin in London with the trial of Thomas Hardy; Habeas Corpus Act suspended in England	First telegraph; Darwin's *Zoonomia*; Paine, *The Age of Reason*; Radcliffe, *Mysteries of Udolpho*; Godwin, *Caleb Williams*
1795	Bread riots in Paris; Speenhamland Act provides poor relief in England; Hastings acquitted	Goethe, *Wilhelm Meisterrs Lehrjahre*; Beethoven, *Opus 1*
1796	Napoleon's Italian Campaign	Wollstonecraft, *Letters Written in Sweden, Norway, and Denmark*; Lewis, *The Monk*; Seward, *Llangollen Vale with Other Poems*

Date	Historical Events	Literature and Science
1797	Napoleon defeats Austrians; Wollstonecraft dies	Radcliffe, *The Italian*; Robinson, *Walsingham; or, the Pupil of Nature;* Hölderlin, *Hyperion*
1798	Napoleon's Egyptian Campaign; Battle of the Nile; Uprising of the United Irishmen, led by Lord Edward Fitzgerald and Wolfe Tone	Wordsworth and Coleridge, *Lyrical Ballads*; Godwin, *Memoirs of Mary Wollstonecraft*; Malthus, *First Essay on the Principle of Population;* Bentham, *Political Economy*; Baillie, *Series of Plays*, vol I
1799	Napoleon's Syrian Campaign, returns to lead coup d'état of Brumaire, becomes First Consul; Edict of Peking bans import of opium into China	Hays, *Victim of Prejudice*; Godwin, *St. Leon*; Wordsworth completes *The Two-Part Prelude*; Beethoven, *Symphony No. 1*; Schlegel, *Lucinde*; Cuvier founds comparative anatomy; Rosetta Stone found in Egypt; preserved mammoth found in Siberia
1800	Renewal of the French Austrian Campaign; Royal Institution of Great Britain founded; Herschel discovers infrared solar rays	Edgeworth, *Castle Rackrent*; Robinson, *Lyrical Tales*; Staël, *De la littérature*; Schelling, *System of Transcendental Idealism*; *The Athenaeum* published; Volta produces electricity from a cell battery

Date	*Historical Events*	*Literature and Science*
1801	Toussaint L'Ouverture takes command of Haiti, liberates enslaved Blacks; Act of Union between Ireland and Gr. Britain; Jefferson becomes 3rd U.S. president; Fulton's submarine *The Nautilus*; first British census	Beethoven, *Moonlight Sonata*; Wordsworth, *Lyrical Ballads (1800)*
1802	Treaty of Amiens between Great Britain, Spain and France; Napoleon becomes Consul for life; *Health and Morals of Apprentices Act* restricts child labor and institutes 12-hr workday	Scott, *Minstrelsy of the Scottish Border*; *Edinburgh Review* founded; *Cobbett's Weekly Political Register* founded
1803	Parthenon frieze sculptures sent to England by Lord Elgin; Fulton uses steam to propel a boat on the Seine	Cobbett, *Parliamentary Debates*
1804	First Empire under Napoleon I; *Code Napoleon* instituted	Schiller, *William Tell*; Taylor, trans. of *The Works of Plato*
1805	Battle of Trafalgar; Boston Athenaeum founded; Mungo Park explores Niger River up to Bussa Rapids	Turner, *The Shipwreck* (painting); Wordsworth completes the 13-book *Prelude*
1806	Holy Roman Empire ends; French wars against Prussia and Russia	Dacre, *Zofloya*
1807	Abolition Act receives royal assent, abolishing the slave trade	Smith, *Beachy Head*; Wordsworth, *Poems in Two Volumes*; Moore, *Irish Melodies*; David, *Coronation of Napoleon* (painting)

Date	*Historical Events*	*Literature and Science*
1808	Covent Garden burns down; excavations at Pompeii	Hunt, *The Examiner* founded; Goethe, *Faust I*; Beethoven, *Symphony No.* 5 and *No.* 6; Dalton, *New System of Chemical Philosophy*
1809	Drury Lane burns down; Madison elected 4th US president; Metternich becomes Austrian Foreign Minister	*The Quarterly Review* founded; Lamark *Philosophie zoologique*; Deluc, *An Elementary Treatise on Geology*
1810	Joseph Bonaparte abandons Madrid; reform bill introduced in Parliament; Wellington defeats French at Salamanca	*Encyclopedia Britannica*, 4th ed.; Staël, *De l'Allemagne*; Goya, *Los Desastres de la Guerra* (engravings)
1811	Geo. III recognized as insane, Prince of Wales declared Regent; First Luddite riots in Nottingham; Nash designs Regent Street, London	Austen, *Sense and Sensibility*
1812	America declares war on Britain; Napoleon's army occupies Moscow; the burning of Moscow by Russians, French retreat	Brothers Grimm, *Fairy Tales*; Goya, *Portrait of the Duke of Wellington* (painting); Beethoven, *Symphony No.* 7 and *No.* 8; Edgeworth, *The Absentee*; Turner, *Hannibal Crossing the Alps* (painting)
1813	Southey becomes poet laureate; Bolívar becomes dictator of Venzuela	Austen, *Pride and Prejudice*; Southey, *Life of Nelson*
1814	Napoleon defeated at Toulouse and exiled to Elba	Austen, *Mansfield Park*; Scott, *Waverley*; Burney, *The Wanderer*

Date	*Historical Events*	*Literature and Science*
1815	Napoleon escapes Elba, defeated at Waterloo, exiled to Saint Helena; Biedermeier style for interior décor begins	Canova, *The Three Graces* (sculpture); Schlegel, *Lectures on Dramatic Art and Literature*; Cary, trans. of Dante's *Divine Comedy*
1816	Parliamentary Committee on Education for the Poor; secular education introduced into India; British missionaries sent to South Africa; Brewster invents kaleidoscope	Austen, *Emma*
1817	James Monroe elected 5th US president	Moore, *Lalla Rookh*; Hazlitt, *Charactes in Shakespeare's Plays*; Scott, *Rob Roy*; Martin, *The Bard* (painting); Hegel, *Encyclopedia of the Philosophical Sciences*
1818	Habeas Corpus restored; Allied forces leave France	M. Shelley, *Frankenstein*; PB Shelley, *Revolt of Islam*; Byron, *Beppo* and *Childe Harold* IV; Keats, *Endymion*; Austen, *Northanger Abbey* and *Persuasion*; Scott, *Heart of Midlothian*
1819	Bolívar becomes President and military dictator of Colombia; Peterloo Massacre, Manchester; East India Company establishes settlement in Singapore; Oersted discovers electromagnetism	Polidori, "The Vampyre"; Byron, *Don Juan* I-II; PB Shelley, *The Cenci*; Combe, *Essays on Phrenology*; Géricault, *Raft of the Medusa* (painting); Wilson, *Sanskrit-English Dictionary*

Date	*Historical Events*	*Literature and Science*
1820	Cato Street Conspiracy; Geo. III dies, Regent becomes George IV; discovery of the *Venus de Milo;* Final Act of Congress of Vienna	Keats, *Lamia, Isabella, the Eve of St Agnes, and other Poems*; Scott, *Ivanhoe*; Maturin, *Melmoth the Wanderer*; Malthus, *Principles of Political Economy*; Ampere, *Laws of Electrodynamic Action*
1821	Greek War of Independence begins; Champollion deciphers Ancient Egyptian hieroglyphs; illicit opium trade in China transferred from Canton to Lintin Island; Sierra Leone, the Gold Coast, and Gambia joined as British West African Settlements	De Quincey, *Confessions of an English Opium-Eater*, pt. 1; Byron, *Sardanapalus*, *The Two Foscari, Cain*; Goethe, *Wilhelm Meisters Wanderjahre*
1822	Turks invade Greece; suicide of Castlereagh; Royal Academy of Music founded (British); Daguerre and Bouton invent the diorama; Britain imports 22,000 pounds of opium	M. Shelley, *Valperga*; Hemans, *The Siege of Valencia;* Pushkin, *Eugen Onegin*; Stendhal, *De l'amour;* Schubert, *Unfinished Symphony*; Delacroix, *Dante and Virgil Crossing the Styx* (painting)
1823	Main façade of British Museum designed; Cauchy establishes fundamental theorem of calculus	Medical journal *The Lancet* founded
1824	British workers permitted to unionize	PB Shelley's *Posthumous* Poems, ed. by M. Shelley
1825	Turks take Missolonghi; Greeks under British protection; Nash remodels Buckingham Palace	Hazitt, *The Spirit of the Age*; Ackerman's gift book *Forget-me-not*

Date	Historical Events	Literature and Science
1826		M. Shelley, *The Last Man*; Disraeli, *Vivian Gray*; Cooper, *Last of the Mohicans*; Martin, *The Deluge* (painting)
1827	Greek independence ensured	Baedeker's first travel guides; Balzac begins *La Comédie humaine*; Audubon begins publishing *Birds of North America*
1828	First professor of English Language and Literature appointed, University of London; Russia declares war on Turkey	Dumas, *Les Trois Mousquetaires*; Webster, *American Dictionary of the English Language*
1829	Catholic Emancipation Act; July Revolution in France	Knapp, *Lectures on American Literature*
1830	George IV dies; Louis Phillipe begins reign in France; Royal Geographic Society founded; steam cars used in London; Liverpool-Manchester Railway opened	Cobbett, *Rural Rides*; Delacroix, *Liberty Leading the People* (painting); Stendhal, *Le Rouge et le Noir*; Moore, *Life of Byron*

INDEX

Page numbers in **bold** indicate tables.

For Product Safety Concerns and Information please contact our EU representative GPSR@taylorandfrancis.com
Taylor & Francis Verlag GmbH, Kaufingerstraße 24, 80331 München, Germany

www.ingramcontent.com/pod-product-compliance
Lightning Source LLC
LaVergne TN
LVHW020847180926
848329LV00027B/292
9781032625690